First World War
and Army of Occupation
War Diary
France, Belgium and Germany

18 DIVISION
Divisional Troops
80 Field Company Royal Engineers
1 January 1916 - 30 April 1919

WO95/2027/2

The Naval & Military Press Ltd
www.nmarchive.com
Published in association with The National Archives

Published by

The Naval & Military Press Ltd

Unit 10 Ridgewood Industrial Park,

Uckfield, East Sussex,

TN22 5QE England

Tel: +44 (0) 1825 749494

www.naval-military-press.com

www.nmarchive.com

This diary has been reprinted in facsimile from the original. Any imperfections are inevitably reproduced and the quality may fall short of modern type and cartographic standards.

© **Crown Copyright**
Images reproduced by permission of The National Archives, London, England, 2015.

Contents

Document type	Place/Title	Date From	Date To
Heading	WO95/2027/2		
Heading	18th Division 8th Field Coy. R.E, Jly 1915-Apl 1919		
Heading	80th Field Company R.E		
Heading			
Miscellaneous			
War Diary			
Miscellaneous			
Miscellaneous	DAAG (1) Forwarded as this is apparently as Original Copy	04/03/1916	04/03/1916
Miscellaneous	O.C. 80th Field Co R.E.	02/03/1916	02/03/1916
Miscellaneous	To C.R.E. 18th Division.	09/08/1916	09/08/1916
War Diary		01/07/1916	01/07/1916
Miscellaneous			
War Diary		01/07/1916	01/07/1916
War Diary	Carnoy	01/07/1916	01/07/1916
War Diary	A.12.C.7.7.	01/07/1916	01/07/1916
Miscellaneous			
War Diary	St Jans Capelle.	01/08/1916	05/08/1916
War Diary	Ref Sheet 36 N.W.6.B. H.6.b.7.0. H.9.b.3.7.	05/08/1916	07/08/1916
War Diary	Rue Marle	15/08/1916	25/08/1916
War Diary	La Thieuloye	26/08/1916	31/08/1916
Heading	18th Div. 80th F.C.R.E. Vol 7		
War Diary	Meauzte	01/01/1916	31/01/1916
Heading	80 F.C.R.E. Vol 4		
War Diary	Meaulte	01/02/1916	02/02/1916
War Diary	La Houssoye	03/02/1916	04/02/1916
War Diary	Naours	05/02/1916	06/02/1916
Heading	80th Field Coy R.E. Vol 8		
War Diary	Naours	07/02/1916	08/03/1916
War Diary	Corbie	11/03/1916	11/03/1916
War Diary	Bray	12/03/1916	31/03/1916
War Diary	La Thieuloye	01/09/1916	17/09/1916
War Diary	Rue Marle	05/08/1916	14/08/1916
War Diary	Raincheval	18/09/1916	20/09/1916
War Diary	Lealvillers	21/09/1916	21/09/1916
War Diary	Martinsart	22/09/1916	05/10/1916
War Diary	Hedauville	06/10/1916	06/10/1916
War Diary	Epecamps & Raincheval	07/10/1916	07/10/1916
War Diary	Epecamps	08/10/1916	15/10/1916
War Diary	Beauval	16/10/1916	16/10/1916
War Diary	Contay	17/10/1916	17/10/1916
War Diary	Bouzincourt	18/10/1916	19/10/1916
War Diary	Ovillers Laboiselle Usna Hill	20/10/1916	30/11/1916
War Diary	Ovillers La Boiselle	01/12/1916	31/12/1916
War Diary	Ouville Chateau	01/01/1917	01/01/1917
War Diary	Ouville	01/01/1917	01/01/1917
War Diary	Abbeville Area.	01/01/1917	02/01/1917
War Diary	Ouville.	03/01/1917	10/01/1917
War Diary	Fransu	11/01/1917	11/01/1917
War Diary	Gorges	12/01/1917	13/01/1917

Type	Description	Start	End
War Diary	Val de Maison	14/01/1917	14/01/1917
War Diary	Martinsart	15/01/1917	15/01/1917
War Diary	X.2.a.2.2.	16/01/1917	22/01/1917
War Diary	Coy Hem X.2.a.2.2.	23/01/1917	21/02/1917
War Diary	Coy Hem W.9.b.8.5.	22/02/1917	28/02/1917
Miscellaneous	Weekly progress report. Appendix A	03/02/1917	03/02/1917
Miscellaneous	Weekly progress report.	09/02/1917	09/02/1917
Miscellaneous	Appendix C. Instructions for R.E Section with regard to Carrying tools etc.	14/01/1917	14/01/1917
War Diary	C.R.E 18 Div from O.C 80 Fd Coy R.E. Appendix D.		
Miscellaneous	80th Fd Coy R.E Order for 17.2.17 and attached Infantry platoons of 54th Inf Bde. Appendix E.		
Miscellaneous	C.R.E 18th Div from O.C 80th Fd Coy R.E Appendix F	23/02/1917	23/02/1917
Miscellaneous	C.R.E 18th Division from OC 80th Fd Coy RE Appendix G	02/03/1917	02/03/1917
Miscellaneous	Weekly progress report 80th Fd Coy RE Week ending 9.3.17 Appendix H		
War Diary	Coy H.Q. W.9.b.8.5.	01/03/1917	01/03/1917
War Diary	Coy H.Q. W.6.c.0.4	02/03/1917	11/03/1917
War Diary	Coy H.Q. R.9.b.5.3	12/03/1917	16/03/1917
War Diary	Coy H.Q. R.5.a.8.1.	17/03/1917	18/03/1917
War Diary	Coy H.Q. G 17 Central	19/03/1917	20/03/1917
War Diary	Coy H.Q. W.6.c.0.4.	21/03/1917	21/03/1917
War Diary	Coy H.Q. Vadencourt	22/03/1917	22/03/1917
War Diary	Montonvillers	23/03/1917	23/03/1917
War Diary	Dury	24/03/1917	24/03/1917
War Diary	Saleux Railway Station	26/03/1917	27/03/1917
War Diary	Gaubecque	28/03/1917	31/03/1917
War Diary	Bray	01/04/1917	29/04/1917
War Diary		28/04/1917	30/04/1917
War Diary	Guarbecque (Pas de Calais).	01/04/1917	20/04/1917
War Diary	Busnes (Pas de Calais)	21/04/1917	25/04/1917
War Diary	Pressy Les Pernes.	26/04/1917	27/04/1917
War Diary	Neauvill Vitasse and Bearains	28/04/1917	28/04/1917
War Diary	N.26.C.0.5.	29/04/1917	01/05/1917
War Diary	New Heninel	01/05/1917	07/05/1917
War Diary	H.Q. L.9.c.4.2.	01/05/1917	01/05/1917
War Diary	Bray.	01/05/1917	31/05/1917
War Diary	H.Q.	01/06/1917	30/06/1917
War Diary	Coy Hqrs & 4 Section	01/06/1917	01/06/1917
War Diary	N 26 Horsel Lines N.25.d.9.5.	02/06/1917	16/06/1917
War Diary	Gaudiempre	17/06/1917	21/06/1917
War Diary	Devonshire Camp	21/06/1917	21/06/1917
War Diary	Ouderdom	22/06/1917	22/06/1917
War Diary	Sheet 28 NW H.26.b Central.	23/06/1917	30/06/1917
War Diary		28/05/1917	28/05/1917
War Diary		03/05/1917	03/05/1917
Miscellaneous	Headquarters, 18th Division.	05/08/1916	05/08/1916
War Diary	Sheet 28 N.W.	01/07/1917	27/07/1917
War Diary		08/05/1917	27/05/1917
War Diary	Sheet 28 N.W. Coy H.Q H.33.b.	01/08/1917	31/08/1917
War Diary		25/07/1917	31/07/1917
War Diary	Ronssoy	29/09/1917	30/09/1917
War Diary	Petit Parann Le Paradis	01/09/1917	03/09/1917
War Diary	Ledringhem	04/09/1917	27/09/1917

War Diary	Coy H.Q. B.22.d.8.1.	28/09/1917	30/09/1917
War Diary	Sheet 28. N.W. Coy H Qrs B.22.d.8.1. Transport at A.21.a.8.7.	01/10/1917	31/10/1917
War Diary	Sheet 28 N.W. Coy H Qrs T Dismounts at C.13.a.19. Transport at B.B.b.8.4.	01/11/1917	30/11/1917
War Diary	Coy B.6.c.8.2.	01/12/1917	01/12/1917
War Diary	Sheet 28	02/12/1917	02/12/1917
War Diary	Transport B.13.b.8.4.	03/12/1917	31/12/1917
War Diary	X.13.a.3.0 Sheet 19	01/01/1918	23/01/1918
War Diary	B.6.c.8.2. Sheet 20.	23/01/1918	31/01/1918
War Diary	Sheet 19 X.13.c.8.2	01/02/1918	09/02/1918
War Diary	St Quentin 1/100,000.	10/02/1918	19/02/1918
War Diary	St Quentin	19/02/1918	28/02/1918
Heading	18th Div. 80th Field Company R.E. March 1918		
War Diary	Commenchon St Quentin 1/100,000	01/03/1918	10/03/1918
War Diary	Rouez.	10/03/1918	31/03/1918
Heading	18th Div 80th Field Company R.E. April 1918		
War Diary	Gentelles Amiens 1/100,000	01/04/1918	24/04/1918
War Diary	Avelesges Dieppe 1/100,000	26/04/1918	30/04/1918
War Diary	Avelesges Coy H.Q at ? c.6.4 Sheet 62.E	01/05/1918	05/05/1918
War Diary	Ray 6	06/05/1918	31/05/1918
War Diary	Warloy Coy Hqrs at V.24.a.6.4. Sheet 57.D.	01/06/1918	28/07/1918
War Diary	Heilly	29/07/1918	31/07/1918
Heading	18th Division Engineers 80th Field Company R.E. August 1918		
War Diary	Heilly	01/08/1918	10/08/1918
War Diary	Warloy Coy Hqrs at V.24.a.6.4. (57 D)	10/08/1918	13/08/1918
War Diary	Warloy	14/08/1918	23/08/1918
War Diary	Lavieville	24/08/1918	28/08/1918
War Diary	Sheet 57c 1/40,000 Bernafy Wood.	28/08/1918	30/08/1918
War Diary	Compres.	30/08/1918	31/08/1918
War Diary	Bernafay Wood.	01/09/1918	02/09/1918
War Diary	Combles	03/09/1918	06/09/1918
War Diary	Aizicourt-Le-Bas.	12/09/1918	23/09/1918
War Diary	Combles	24/09/1918	27/09/1918
War Diary	Nurlu	27/09/1918	02/10/1918
War Diary	Beaucourt Sur Hallue	03/10/1918	16/10/1918
War Diary	Nurlu	17/10/1918	17/10/1918
War Diary	Serain	18/10/1918	20/10/1918
War Diary	Maurois	21/10/1918	21/10/1918
War Diary	Le Cateau	22/10/1918	07/11/1918
War Diary	Hachette	08/11/1918	30/11/1918
War Diary	Serain.	01/12/1918	10/12/1918
War Diary	Walincourt.	11/12/1918	31/12/1918
War Diary	Walincourt.	01/02/1919	31/03/1919
War Diary	Caudry.	01/04/1919	30/04/1919

WO95/2027/2

18TH DIVISION

80TH FIELD COY. R.E.

JLY 1915 – APL 1919.

80TH
FIELD COMPANY R.E.

WAR DIARY

INTELLIGENCE SUMMARY

WAR DIARY / INTELLIGENCE SUMMARY

Army Form C. 2118

Place	Date	Hour	Summary of Events and Information	Remarks and references to Appendices
Sandhill Camp	Oct 1915		The Battalion used in the Brickstacks to assist the Engineers whose number very between six and a dozen occupying to prevent wastage of water. The Eastward point of known as "No 8" line staying was K each shift; relieved the Bryce Bourne the Saxonist being lifted during hours of darkness by the Pontoon sand light fender for general use. Belonging to the Company. Two 30 inch Sumps were provided into the bank and bars being chained by the Sappers when on duty. Cleaning out and disinfecting as well done by the French land. 2" to 1" mains laid. Pump erected. Tanks fitted for water supply work to static with K Battalion Head Quarters. Trench pickets being made from [?] for posts.	

Daalen.

Forwarded as this is apparently an original copy.

6/8/16

JW Davison
Lieut
RE KRRC

4/3

From.
O.C. 80th Field Co. R.E.

To
CRE XVIII Div.

Herewith please find attached
War Diary of movements
work of my Company for the
past month.

H Chambers
Capt RE

O.C. 80th Field Co. R.E.

D.A.G. R.E. Section
Base.

Forwarded.

H.G. Salbury
Lt Col RE
CRE. 18° Div.

2.3.16.

To C.R.E.
     18th Division.

Enclosed are sketches indicating points, etc, mentioned in the WAR DIARY of the above Coy for month ending July. 31. 1916, which was forwarded to you on the 5th inst.

            [signature]
         O.C. 80th Field Co. R.E.

WAR DIARY
or
INTELLIGENCE SUMMARY

Army Form C. 2118

Place	Date	Hour	Summary of Events and Information	Remarks and references to Appendices
July	1st	7.30 am	80th Coy. H.Q. A.13.d.6.9. Zero hour.	See 1.
			No. 2 and 4 Section in CARNOY, & Nos 11 and 12 Platoon 8th R. Sussex Pioneers attached	
			No 1 Section BRAY 2.9.a.4.2	
			No 3 Section H.Q. at BRONFAY FARM for maintenance of SUZANNE - CARNOY water supply.	
			Transport L.14.b.7.8.	
			O.C. 80th Coy. (Bt Oppur.) No 1.	
			With reference to 96 in. Bde. Preliminary Op. Order No. 17 & order 3 of order No 1.	
			No 11 Platoon 8th R. Sussex Pioneers under Lieut Copper and No 2 Section R.E. under Lieut Knipe R.E. will leave the Bde dug-outs at F.18.c.9.5. in the order named 1 hour after zero and proceed to an advanced strong point not under	
			Pioneer	
			Sapper III IV V	
			Both parties will move in rear of 6th R. Northants	
			Lieut Copper placed for in. forces into O.C. B Coy 8th Batt. Northants and Lieut Knipe R.E. with O.C. A Coy 8th Batt. Northants	
			No 2 Section R.E. and four Bremen RE and No 12 Platoon 8th R. Sussex Pioneers under Capt Ireland will be ready to move off from F.18.c.9.9. at 15 hours after zero and will proceed to consolidate BEETLE ALLEY and a forward strong point on the final objective	
			This party will set part the line ROAD TRENCH until BEETLE ALLEY	

WAR DIARY
or
INTELLIGENCE SUMMARY
(Erase heading not required.)

Army Form C. 2118

Place	Date	Hour	Summary of Events and Information	Remarks and references to Appendices
50th Field Coy RE			is captured, and will not go forward of PORNIER TRENCH until	
			objective is gained. On arrival at BEETLE ALLEY the three parties	
			proceed to consolidate it under their Section Commanders	
			Officers and N.C.O's will proceed to reconnoitre the front objective as	
			the situation permits. He will then send back of the remainder of	
			No 2 Section and may call on 1st Ireland of help to hold trench	
			fill. A detached party forming will be used entirely for carrying	
			No 1 Section under Lieut Viger will be in DIVISIONAL RESERVE and	
			will parade at BRAY at two hours after zero and proceed to CARNOY.	
			Tools (a) Shovel per man	
			(b) Being stores man 2 picks.	
			(c) This will be carried in proportion of	
			3 men for hand grenades	
			8 " " bizkets will carry 2/2	
			6 " " barbed wire	
			10 " " panels wire	
			They must be made with sandbags and drawn from CARNOY on	
			Y day	
			Dress Rifle and Equipment less pack	Carrying with Every ration
			No Pouches G.S.A	1 day prophet
			Haversack with one days ration + 1 iron ration	jersey
				Two Smoke helmets
				Two Sandbags

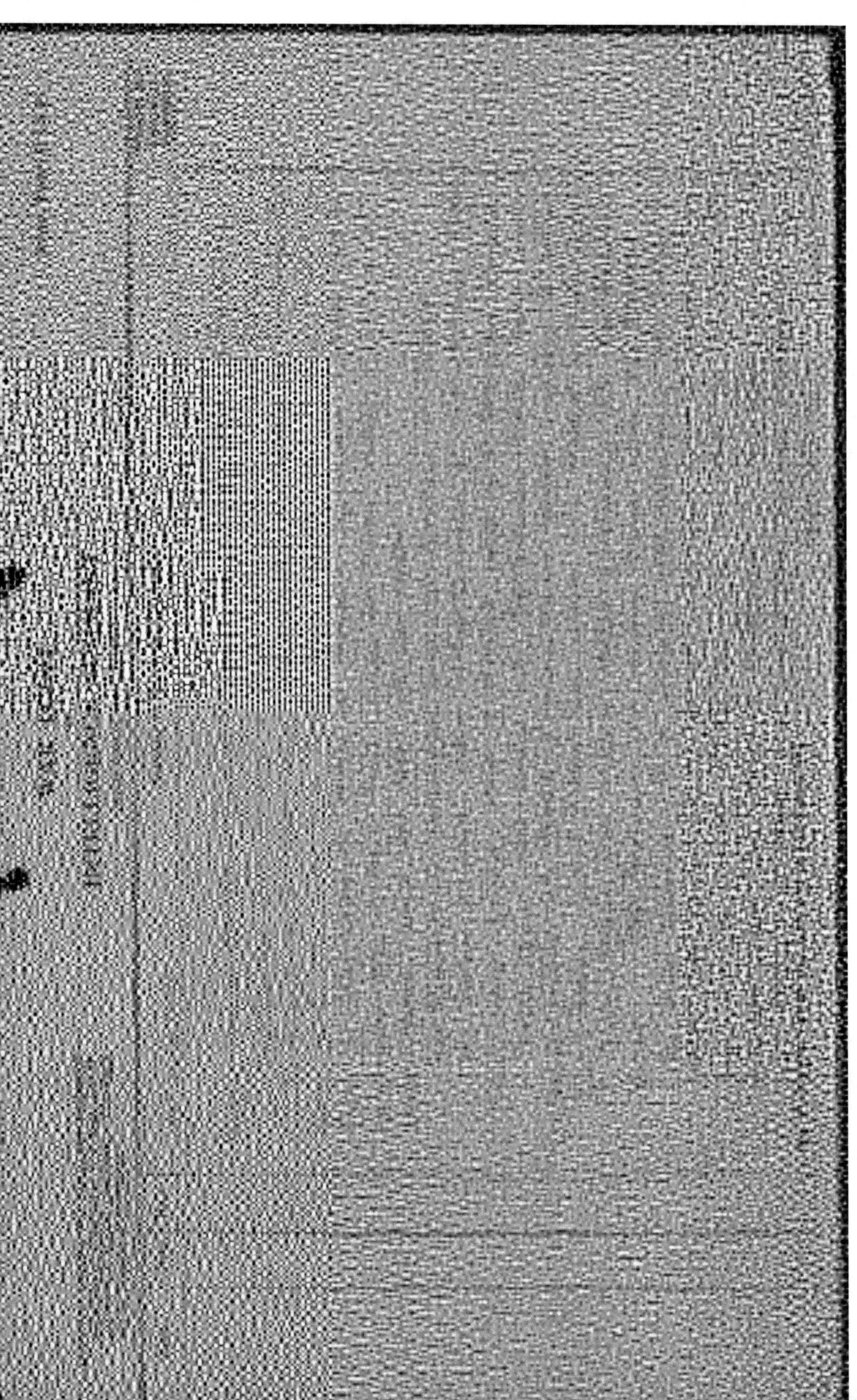

WAR DIARY
or
INTELLIGENCE SUMMARY

Army Form C. 2118

(Erase heading not required.)

folio 6

Place	Date	Hour	Summary of Events and Information	Remarks and references to Appendices
	1-7-16	6.55pm cont'd	At this time WHITE TRENCH was only occupied up to S 26 c.2.8 on VIIth Division had not occupied their portion of this Trench.	
		8pm 7pm	Capt CHASE ordered Lieut Brennen to proceed to & occupy WHITE TRENCH & if possible POMMIERS REDOUBT because it seemed doubtful if the VIIth Divn would occupy WHITE TRENCH in 17·16	
			At this time it was possible to walk over the open from POMMIERS REDOUBT to S25 b 5.1 without coming under rifle or shell fire. No enemy appears to be in WHITE TRENCH at all	
		9pm	No 2+ Section having completed the Technical work of wiring the string points VI + VII (POMMIERS REDOUBT) relieved No 4. the TRIANGLE for h of trend. S15 D 9.4	(POMMLERS REDOUBT)
CARNOY	1·7·16	11.15am	No 1 section under Lieut Vigors RE arrived at R.E. DUMP from CARNOY, and was employed in making up man loads of turns and pickets, and lorry turning material for 4 pack animals of this company that arrived from BRAY.	S15 D 9.4
		noon	Capt Chase wired to 54 + 138e asking for permission tree no 1 section, which was in divisional reserve, for the purpose of opening brides men on in front his trenches in the valley A18 a 3.7. – S7 b 38. 3 Pack animals started up to TRIANGLE with mining material and Capt GREEN R.E.	S16 b 29.
		1.15pm	Permission allowed tree no 1 section which started forward into Stanton wagon tree of digging material for men of his trenches at A12 c 77	
		2pm	Capt CHASE arrived and took Enemy started heavy of the valley A18 a 3.7 S 7 b 3.8 particularly at A12 c 7.7 with 4.2 Howitzer shells.	

1875 Wt. W593/826 1,000,000 4/15 J.B.C. & A. A.D.S.S./Forms/C. 2118.

Army Form C. 2118

WAR DIARY
or
INTELLIGENCE SUMMARY
(Erase heading not required.)

folio 7

Place	Date	Hour	Summary of Events and Information	Remarks and references to Appendices
A 12 c 7.7	1-7-16	2.15pm	Lieut Vigers killed – Difficulty experienced in unloading pontoon wagons and carrying on work owing to enemy fire. Pontoon wagon were not visible to enemy who had been driven near ROAMIER'S RIDGE.	
		2.25pm	5 men casualties from shell fire dropped under the pontoon wagon, 2 horses ― Decided to offload pontoon wagons where they stood & send them away.	
		2.45pm	Handed over work to Sergt. NEWBERY, took a guide to common front line & located & fill in which at that spot near A 7 b 5.7. Sent guide back to indicate spot to Sergt Newbery	
		7.30	2nd went on to TRIANGLE	
		10.40pm	[illegible] TRIANGLE completed	
		1.15pm (?)	3 Pontoon Wagons full of pioneer material arrived at the [illegible]	
		3pm	Packhorses with wire material arrived at TRIANGLE, offloaded and returned to CARNOY	
		7.30pm	Packhorses with rations for 2 Belvino arrived at TRIANGLE.	
		10.30pm	Road to TRIANGLE completed	
		11.30pm	3 Pontoon wagons full of pioneer material and 250 gall canvas tank offloaded at TRIANGLE	
			Followed later by 15th TRANSPORT and water cart which filled up to 250 gall canvas tank.	

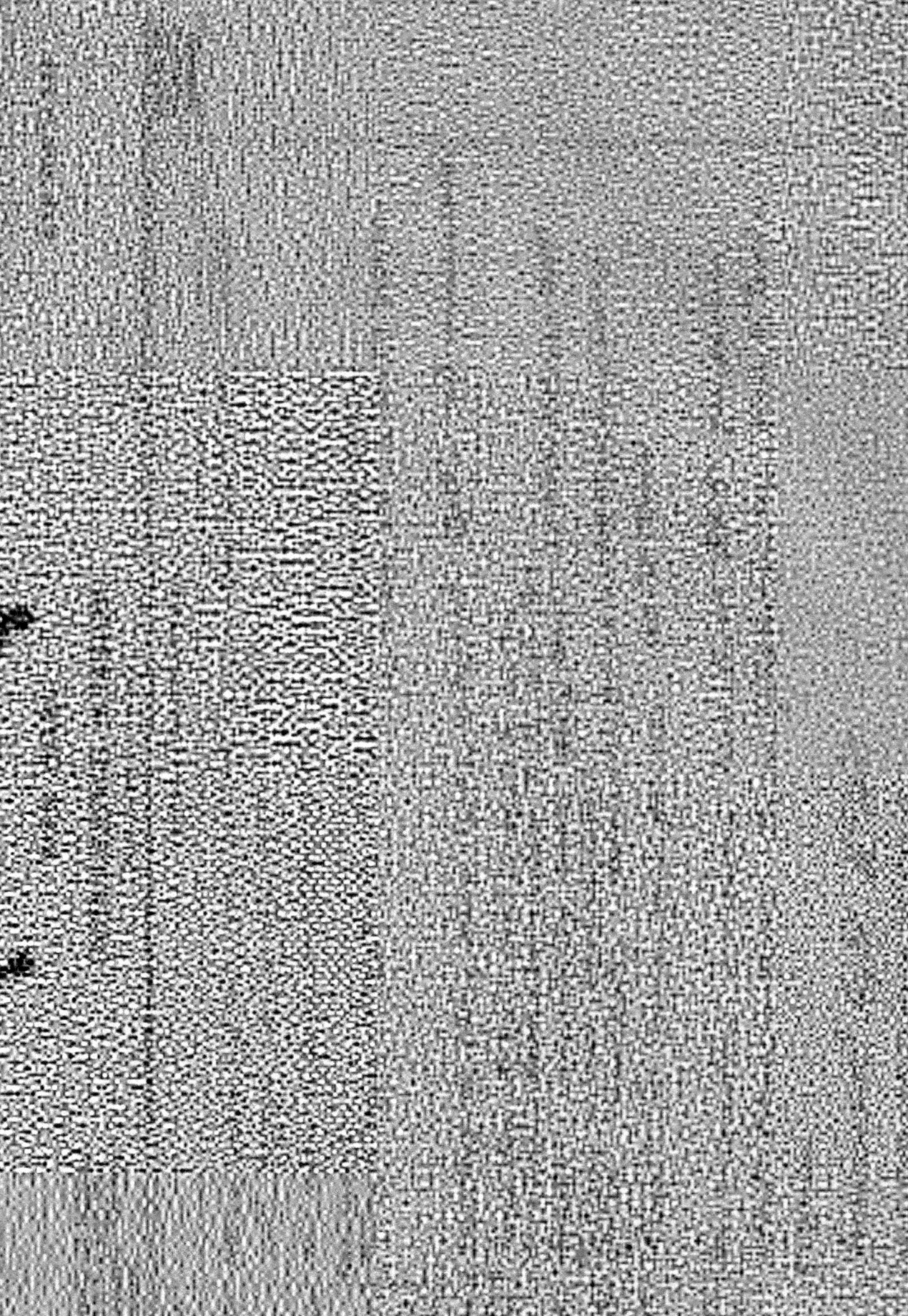

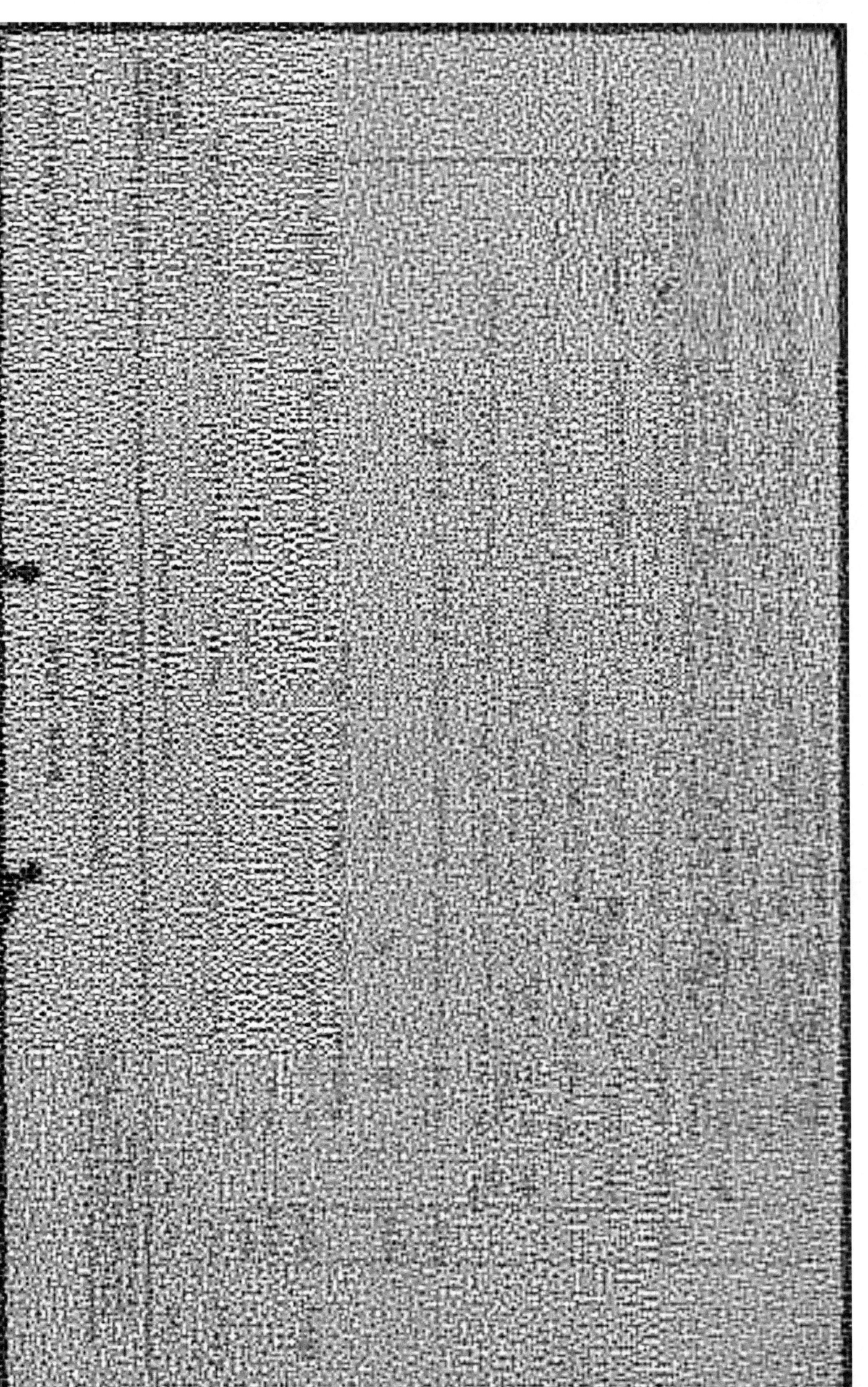

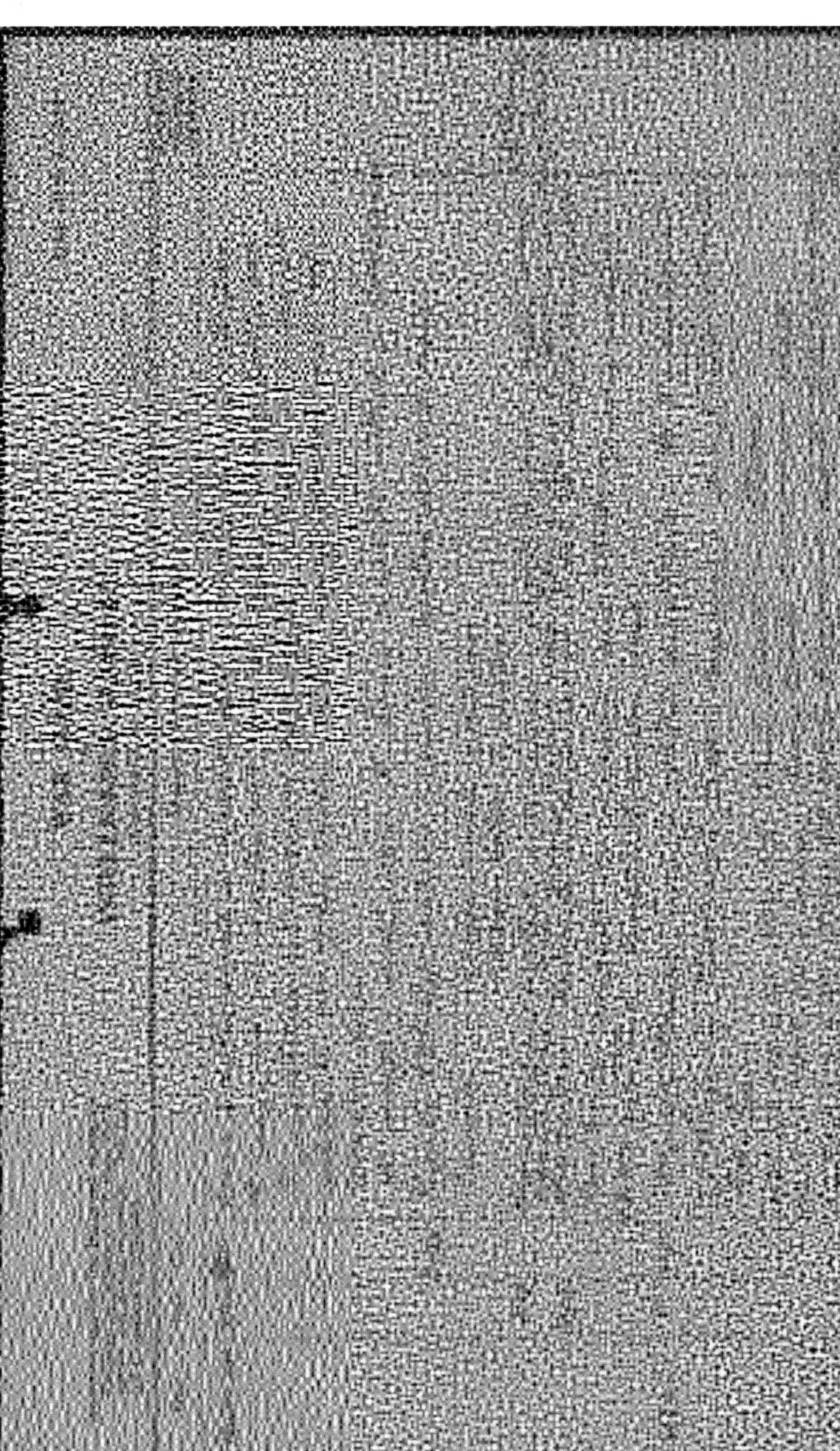

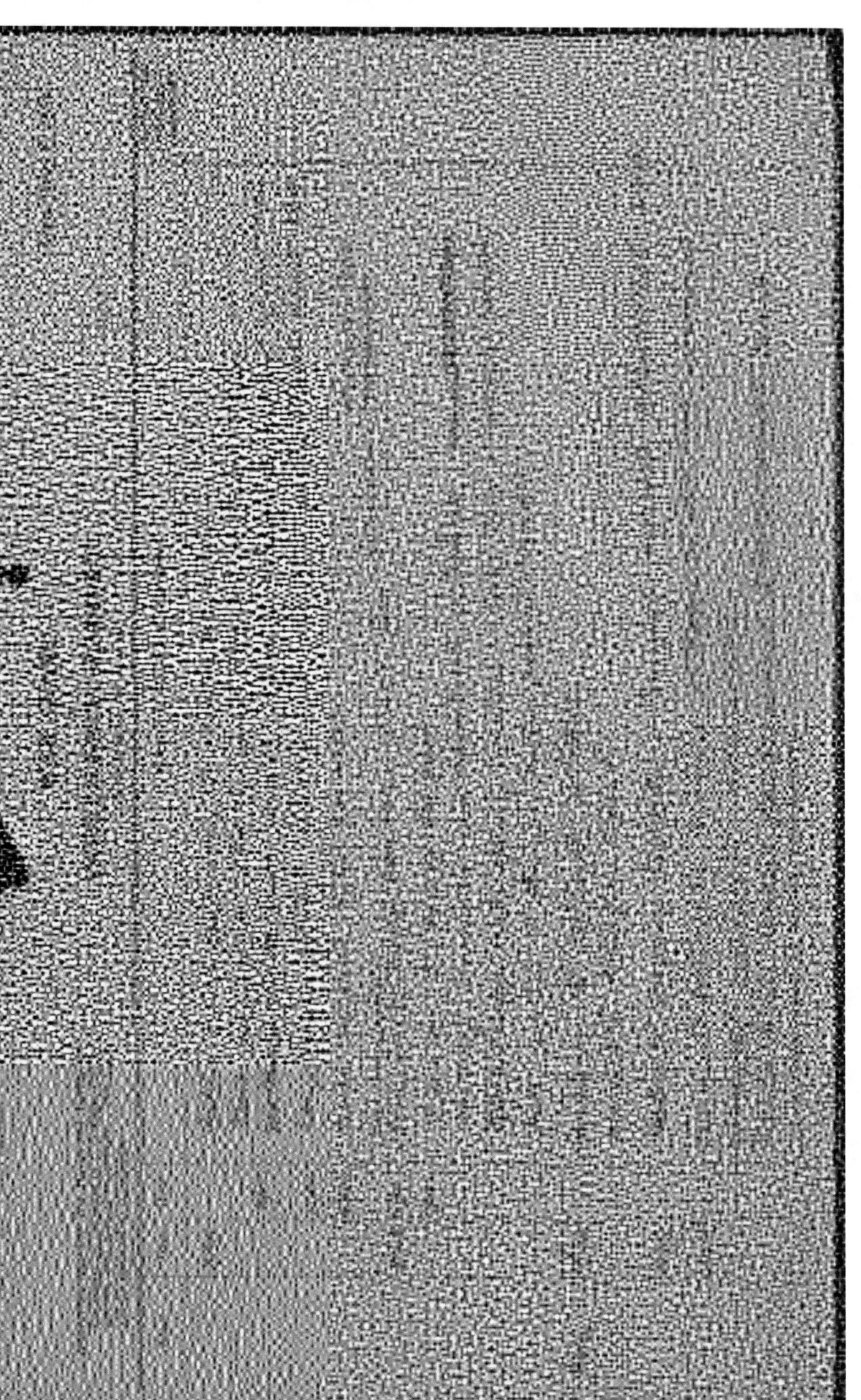

WAR DIARY

INTELLIGENCE SUMMARY

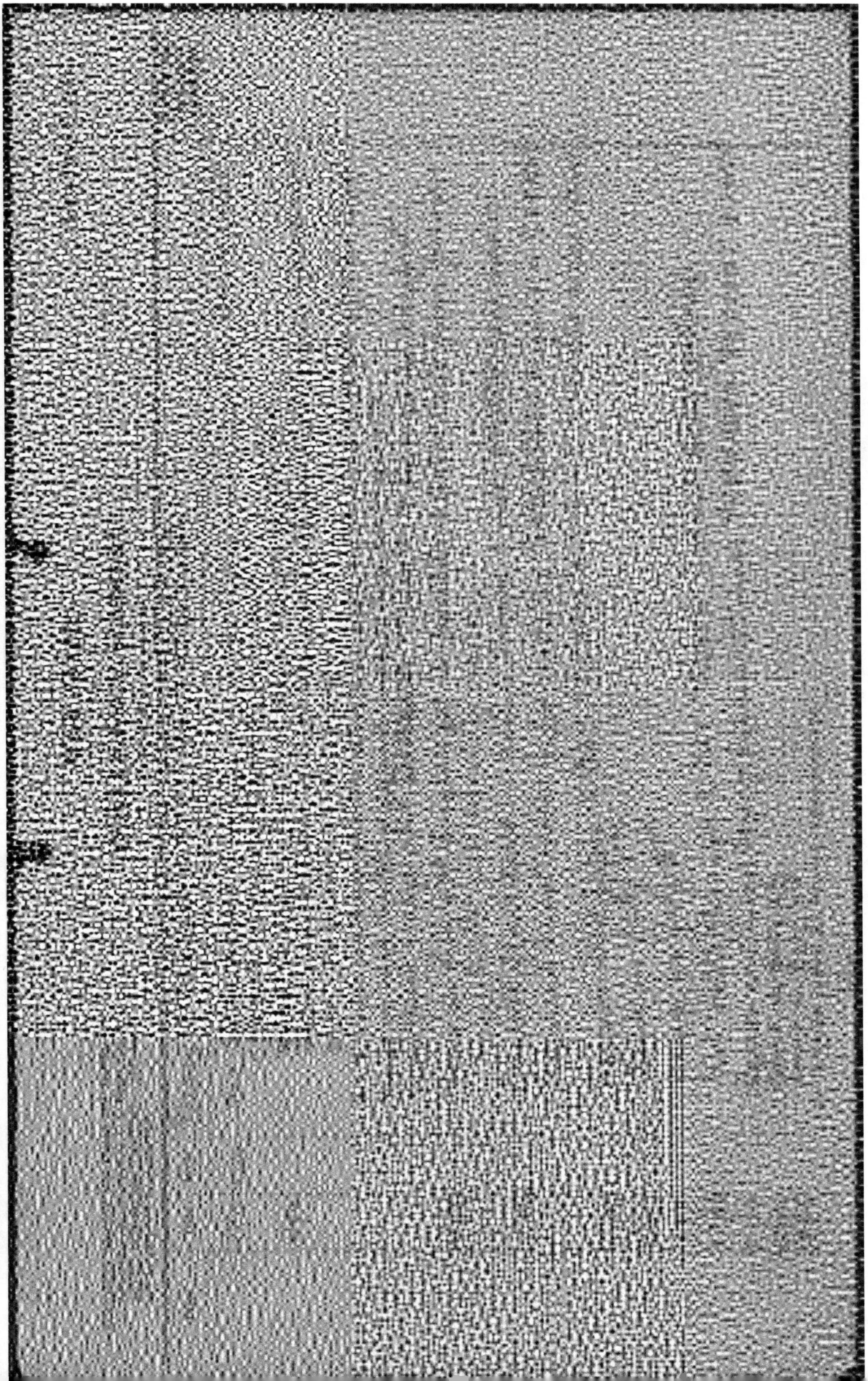

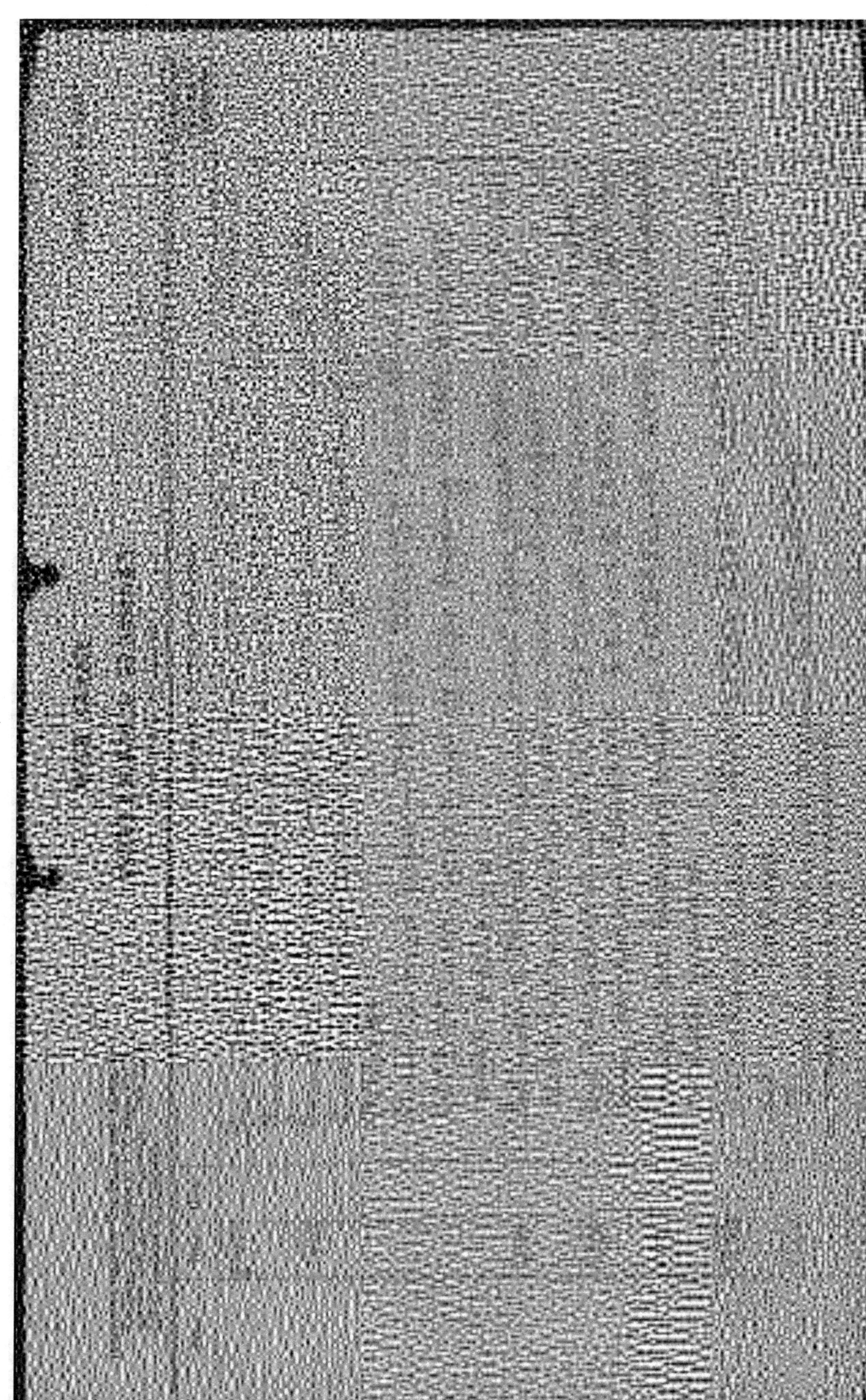

WAR DIARY

INTELLIGENCE SUMMARY

Army Form C. 2118

WAR DIARY
or
INTELLIGENCE SUMMARY

60th Field Coy. R.E. Vol. IX

(Erase heading not required.)

Instructions regarding War Diaries and Intelligence Summaries are contained in F.S. Regs., Part II. and the Staff Manual respectively. Title Pages will be prepared in manuscript.

Place	Date	Hour	Summary of Events and Information August 1916 Folio 1	Remarks and references to Appendices
Ft. JANS CAPELLE	1/8/16		G.O.C. Division inspected Divisional Field Companies Wh.	
	2/8/16		Train in.	
	3/8/16			
	4/8/16			
	5/8/16		Company marched to area S and S.W. of ARMENTIERES.	
Ref. Sheet 36.N.W.6.B.				
H.6.b.4.0. H.9.b.3.7.			Company HQrs. and ammunition Part of company billeted in RUE MASLE Mounted section and transport at ERQUINGHEM.	
	6/8/16		Took over from 1st and 2nd Field Companies New Zealand Engineers on front BOIS-GRENIER Ref. sheet 36.N.W.4 edition 6.B. I.31.c.4.4 to I.20.d.5.3.	
	7/8/16		Part of company had talks. Started work on trenches — Constructing Breastworks, Heavy Tine Relief DEAD COW FARM. REPAIRING and RECONSTRUCTING Shield and Breastwork I.16.C.8.9. Constructing Parados to locality trench I.15.1.	

Syllabi-lectr. Lee 2 & 3.
Lt. Sub. sect. Lee 1 & 4.

M c GuiRE

WAR DIARY
or
INTELLIGENCE SUMMARY

(Erase heading not required.)

Army Form C. 2118

Instructions regarding War Diaries and Intelligence Summaries are contained in F.S. Regs., Part II. and the Staff Manual respectively. Title Pages will be prepared in manuscript.

Summary of Events and Information Aug. 1916 Folio 3

Place	Date	Hour	Summary of Events and Information	Remarks and references to Appendices
Rue Marle	15/8/16		No.4 Section Training	
			No.2 Sect. " Reconstructing WILLOW AVENUE & front line in SALIENT.	
			No.3 " " Training	
			No.1 " " Revetting & Rep. trench in MINERS LANE & left of COWGATE AVENUE	
"	16/8/16		No.1 Sec. Training	
			"2 " Training	
			"3 " Work on WILLOW AVENUE & SALIENT	
			"4 " Work on SALOP AVENUE & MINERS LANE	
"	17/8/16		No.1 do.t Same as 15/8/16	
			" 2 do.t Same as 15/8/16	
			" 3 do.t Training	
			" 4 do.t Training	
"	18/8/16		No.1 do.t Same as 15/8/16	All training in this area was in — consolidation of captured villages.
			" 2 do.t Same as 16/8/16	
			" 3 do.t Training	
			" 4 do.t Training	
"	19/8/16		" 1 do.t Training & night work 7 Sally Ports	
			" 2 do.t Same as 16/8/16	
			" 3 do.t Same as 16/8/16	
			" 4 do.t Training	
"	20/8/16		" 1 do.t Training	
			" 2 do.t Same as 16/8/16	
			" 3 do.t Same as 16/8/16	

H. Wemberly IRE

WAR DIARY
or
INTELLIGENCE SUMMARY

Army Form C. 2118

Summary of Events and Information Aug 1916 Folio 4

Place	Date	Hour	Summary of Events and Information	Remarks and references to Appendices
Rue Marle	21/8/16		No 1 Sec. Revetting flanking trenches west left of AVONDALE AVENUE	
			" 2 " Same as 15/8/16 & clearing RUE DU BOIS	
			" 3 " Same as 16/8/16.	
	22/8/16		" 4 " Same as 20/8/16	
			" 2 " Same as 21/8/16.	
	23/8/16		Company moved to ERQUINGHEM	
	24/8/16		Route March & Baths for Company. Training (in consolidation of villages).	
La Thieuloye	25/8/16		Company marched to BAILLEUL WEST & entrained for ST POL, on arrival marched to LA THIEULOYE	
"	26/8/16		Training ⎫	
"	27/8/16		Training ⎬ mitrailleuse consolidation of trenches	
"	28/8/16		Training ⎭ series of trenches taken.	
"	29/8/16		Practice in infantry taking up the consolidation of trenches woods in conjunction with Machine Gun company.	
"	30/8/16		Training " " consolidation of trenches in	
"	31/8/16		Training conjunction with 54th Bde.	

80th F.C.R.E.
Vol: 47

1st Div.

WAR DIARY
or
INTELLIGENCE SUMMARY
(Erase heading not required.)

Army Form C. 2118

80th Field Coy RE (Picardy D. Sector)

Instructions regarding War Diaries and Intelligence Summaries are contained in F.S. Regs., Part II. and the Staff Manual respectively. Title Pages will be prepared in manuscript.

Place	Date	Hour	Summary of Events and Information	Remarks and references to Appendices
MEAULTE	Jan 1st		Own work continues to revetting and repair of communication and overhead and repair of dugouts in D, and D2 sector. BONTE REDOUBT is being drained. Received six Emplacements under the banks of the FRICOURT-BECORDEL ROAD in front of KINGSTON ROAD. Moving to position these two Emplacements in front of KINGSTON ROAD. Instituted forward dumps of RE material at BECORDEL BRIDGES and CRATES (for use of Battalions in D1 and D2 respectively) also supply of sandbags. The Battalions take thereform the day's supply of sandbags and any such required material or any tools.	
	Jan 2nd		Arrangement must be made for the many little D2 posts	
	Jan 3rd		Reconnaissance for MG. Gun Bedos D2 front line. Other work as before.	
	Jan 4th		Supply of Timber & Company fatigue parties insufficient to saw planks, tow ends to cut out new Timber and lead same on wicket malts posts for D1 and D2.	
	Jan 5th		Road widening Scheme started 71 - RE Pump BERNANCOURT. Instructing Infantry parties in wiring. Still by day and night. Screw post double apron type posts.	Trench mine laid after killing 13th day after

WAR DIARY
or
INTELLIGENCE SUMMARY
(Erase heading not required.)

Army Form C. 2118

Instructions regarding War Diaries and Intelligence Summaries are contained in F.S. Regs., Part II. and the Staff Manual respectively. Title Pages will be prepared in manuscript.

South Field Coy. R.E. (Div. and Dr. Sector)

Place	Date	Hour	Summary of Events and Information	Remarks and references to Appendices
	Jan 6		Carrying on with heavy trench infantry revetting. Wiring party strong.	
	Jan 7		Working as before and also No. 2 Observation Post (X Corps) and No. 4 Survey Post was 3ft shelter 18 feet long for the men's quarters. Sawmill & SPU working 8 and 16 hour respectively.	
	Jan 8		Continued to lay men from R.E. 3 to OP to Reference Dr Beta to avoid men walking in the open. 3 of them caught by H.E. yesterday.	
	Jan 9		(Cooking interest that Dr to 60 ft trench through tomorrow tonight by Infantry. Trench during the last fortnight 200 men an hour train.	
	Jan 10		Wiring carried through tonight full 600' with no casualties and all went well. Workshop building and was full steel shelter for delivery to 66 ft Curtis Power Instrument. Tram on DL of three in Diamond Dr Sector. Tunnel air for long affection rails 18" long trolley suspended from Stout wooden frame nails through 2 ft apart and steel with 3/4" bar.	
	Jan 11		Went with Queston of Recorders defences and more mini Stout infantry revetting in wooden posts were now SPU. Started on 9th complete. 600 + mini	

Army Form C. 2118

WAR DIARY
or
INTELLIGENCE SUMMARY
(Erase heading not required.)

80th Field Coy. (R. and D. Section)

Place	Date	Hour	Summary of Events and Information	Remarks and references to Appendices
	Jan 12		Commenced to improve steering out of BECORDEL RAVINE. Entrance must be made through here as BECORDEL is not healthy in front of the Village for troops.	
	Jan 13		Reconnaissance of D. Sigur front trenches. All others as before.	
	Jan 14		Erection of two R.E. Emplacements for Infantry in Sheeters showing the two necessary types of mounting supplied to R.E. Parks.	
	Jan 15		Nothing of note. Infantry parties [sketch] erecting barbed wire entanglements — free tail forwards. 6ft × 8ft — 15 claw barbed wire	
	Jan 16		Erection of barbed-wire screens to shield Railway (used as communication) leading to Well in D. Sector.	
	Jan 17		The second intended Infantry put up just on 40° south upon sniper's post line in D. Sector. Will 1 casualty.	
	Jan 18		Nothing of note.	
	Jan 19		Ventilating tunnelled dug outs (by boring down from surface) in KINGSTON ROAD. Laying Roadwork in RAVINE from WELL 120× from to communication with General Railway Communication trench	

Army Form C. 2118

WAR DIARY
or
INTELLIGENCE SUMMARY

(Erase heading not required.)

Instructions regarding War Diaries and Intelligence Summaries are contained in F. S. Regs., Part II. and the Staff Manual respectively. Title Pages will be prepared in manuscript.

86th Field Coy R.E. (Diamond Redoubt) (4)

Place	Date	Hour	Summary of Events and Information	Remarks and references to Appendices
	Jan 20th		Commenced arrangements for Boardwalk from Little BRIDGES W of BEGORDEL through RAVINE to SENTRY POST near BEGORDEL BRIDGE. over BEGORDEL - BECOURT road. Tried run on gas bench 10 hours on Boardwalk: 75" run with 75 2-0 sleepers 4 x 7 (18" wide) 3 " 6 x 1" 27 feet run for light shoring 4 x 7 ,, Trench revetting 1 ,, various timber Also 16 trench frames were made 6ft long 18" wide	
	Jan 21st		Improvement to BECORDEL was commenced and work to M.G. Emplacements.	
	Jan 22nd		Commenced laying Boardwalk in BECORDEL RAVINE. Party to BECORDEL " MAPLE REDOUBT All other work in D1 and D2 Sector as usual	
	Jan 23rd		Nothing special to report. laying 1" main from top of RONDEZ AVENUE to KINGSTON ROAD COOKHOUSE. -distance 450".	
	Jan 24th		Nothing special to report	

WAR DIARY
or
INTELLIGENCE SUMMARY

(Erase heading not required.)

Army Form C. 2118

80th Field Coy. (R.E. and R. Sector)

Place	Date	Hour	Summary of Events and Information	Remarks and references to Appendices
	Jan 26 to Jan 28		Work & BONTE Dugout, BLOCKHOUSE, MAPLE REDOUBT REDOUBT. 1" M.C. Emplacements. 1" MAIN & KINGSTON ROAD COOKHOUSE. Boardwalk in BECORDEL RAVINE completed today 600' done 18" wide.	
	Jan 29		Cleaning up works. No Company is to move shortly.	
	Jan 30		150' of boardwalk between BRIDLE PATH & MAIDSTONE AVENUE & 600' of boardwalk laid on the top of MAIDSTONE AVENUE trenches just cleaned sufficiently to permit of the laying and driving of piles.	
			The following is a summary of work carried out by the Company during the month of January.	
			No 1 Section has been attached for work under the CRE. 1680" run of Boardwalk 18" wide laid on sleepers carried on piles. 260" run of trenches in D. Sector have been newly revetted. In addition to general repair. BONTE REDOUBT new trench have been drained and cleaned. 600' new flanked (?) laying supplied to Sutton Veney for RUNDLE AVENUE (D.) and SHOOTERS HILL (B.O.) 700' of newly named MAPLE REDOUBT has been opened and revetted	

1875 Wt. W593/826 1,000,000 4/15 J.B.C. & A. A.D.S.S./Forms/C. 2118.

WAR DIARY
INTELLIGENCE SUMMARY

Army Form C. 2118

80th Field Coy. R.E. (D. and D. 2 Sector) (6)

Place	Date	Hour	Summary of Events and Information	Remarks and references to Appendices
			Summary of work (continued)	
		1000	Four in front of B.2 sector Enacted water R.E. Superintion in relation to siting and necessary reconnaissance between front of ESTAMINET & where 83 STREET leaves the front line.	
		800	3 men in front and around village of PLOEGSTRT. by water authorities of R.E.	
		Cav 18ft	Steel Shelter up to NP 2 Survey Post. NP 1 Observation Posn.	
		12 ft.	ditto	
		12 feet	of ditto to KINGSTON ROAD cookhouse. Filo returned to Offr. Supply and driving for all new and complete posts to R.E Stores Parc[?] for Main Steel Shelter work in KINGSTON ROAD and PARK LANE.	
		A. 16 ft.	Dug out and also Medical Inspection room rebuilt in PARK LANE.	
			Repairs to mine dug out in Pts. 88, 89, 90 Trenches. Officer dug out in BONTE rebuilt. Removing old huts from BONTE dugouts in order to replace with Steel Shelters. 20 feet ---- Steel opened up. Tube shelters to Tunnelled R.E. emplacement in KINGSTON ROAD	

Army Form C. 2118

WAR DIARY
or
INTELLIGENCE SUMMARY
(Erase heading not required.)

90th Field Coy R.E. (D. and D. Section)

Place	Date	Hour	Summary of Events and Information	Remarks and references to Appendices
			Summary of work (continued)	

D.I. left Company Tunnelled Bomb store completed & photo-proof erected at entrance for 80th Division of Bombs.

Pierced repairs & loopholes. Training from CITADEL to D.H.Q.

Construction of M.G. observation post overlooking J.Ricourt for X Corps. Trench support & special periscope in same.

200 yards of fire trench laid between R3 and R3 trench Coy Headquarters Nr.

450 " " " " RUNDLEAKARDE (DIETRO BOUT) and KINGSTON ROAD Concreted cooperate of fifty grappa traps for same.

30x tunnel in D.2 front line near ESTAMINET for Shelter Latrine communication.

280 x run of tornatozan sereens made and erected to screen communication and certain shelter trenches.

Cutting of 270 16ft logs for supply ISLANDRIS.

500 infantry instructed in various types of mining and drill for same.

300x main road widened with gravel & provide a chalk foundation at W. End of DERANCOURT outside the village.

WAR DIARY
or
INTELLIGENCE SUMMARY

Army Form C. 2118

Summary (continued)

Supervision of R.E. Dump DERNANCOURT, and St. 5 Bn [gals] Railway, personal workshop and sawmill.

80th R.E. 35,000 [rounds?] full flights of various sizes have been sent up during the month from above dump.

The wound received [?] that the Company is [in excellent?]
Sickness has been practically nil. Life Casualties. (1 Sapper and 1 driver)
was wounded.

B. Chambers. Lieut Col.

O.C. 80th Field Co. R.E.

9 FEB 1916

80 JER 5 Vol 4

WAR DIARY
or
INTELLIGENCE SUMMARY

Army Form C. 2118

80th Field Coy. R.E.

Place	Date	Hour	Summary of Events and Information	Remarks and references to Appendices
MÉAULTE	Feb	1st	Received orders from CRE XIII DIV. that Company will proceed to LAHOUSSOYE en route for NAOURS to arrive at latter place on the 5th. Company packing up and clearing up. Lieut KNIGHT and party of 15 men proceeded to NAOURS direct by motor lorry as advance party. 1 sec No.4 Section	
"	"	2nd	Handed over R.E. work shops to 92nd R.E. Sappers DALE and HORNE and 80th R.E. will remain at BECKANCOURT to man 92nd R.E. Sawbench will 6 men of R. Sussex Pioneers. All wagons and limbers packed complete by 5 p.m. 1sec No.4 Section	
LAHOUSSOYE	"	3rd	Company left MÉAULTE at 9.40 a.m. and marched to LAHOUSSOYE arriving at latter place at 1.30 p.m. billets rough.	
"	"	4th	Company remained at LAHOUSSOYE this day.	
NAOURS	"	5th	Company left LAHOUSSOYE at 10.15 a.m. and marched to NAOURS arriving at latter village at 4.45 p.m. Billets good.	
"	"	6th	Visited TALMAS and NAOURS with CAPT CROMP R.E. (5th G.S. Coy R.E.) with reference to work to be done. Lieut KNIGHT to TALMAT & VIGERS to WARGNIES WARGNIES } re work to be done and HAVERNAT	

18ch

88ch. Field Coy R.E.

Vol III

8

Army Form C. 2118

WAR DIARY
or
INTELLIGENCE SUMMARY
(Erase heading not required.)

Instructions regarding War Diaries and Intelligence Summaries are contained in F. S. Regs., Part II. and the Staff Manual respectively. Title Pages will be prepared in manuscript.

Folio 2.
80th Field Coy RE.

Place	Date	Hour	Summary of Events and Information	Remarks and references to Appendices
NAOURI	Feb 7th		No 2 Section under LIEUT KNIGHT proceeded to TAHMAR to repair those standings in NAOURI.	
"		3	commenced work to repair & erection of those standings in NAOURI.	
"		15.15	No 1 Section under The CRE XVII DIV for work at RIBEMONT under 2/LIEUT VICKERS to WARGNIES for work 18. Billets	
"	8th		No 2 Section to foundations for Well Pumps and repair to Billets	
"		3	"	
"		1	CE X Corps visited office this afternoon.	
"	9		All as before. Remo: 1 Officer change and 1 L.D. transferred to 30th M.V.S.	
"	10	12	" reclassified by D.D.G. 7th L.D.	
"	11	12	All as before	
"			All as before.	
"	12th		All as before : weekly report forwarded. Sent to CRE XVII DIV/Company field.	
"	13th		All as before working half day. New baking afternoon.	
"	14		All as before.	
"	15th		All as before.	
"	16th		All as before; Stone from NERICOURT No 6 RE PARK for works in hand Capt CE X Corps/Office and another here. Part 13th Section at BUIRE.	
"	17		All as before. Bought clinker to fame for redo cube for top sheets of have standing. A dusbelier to lorry (Stan)	

Army Form C. 2118

WAR DIARY
or
INTELLIGENCE SUMMARY
(Erase heading not required.)

Instructions regarding War Diaries and Intelligence Summaries are contained in F.S. Regs., Part II. and the Staff Manual respectively. Title Pages will be prepared in manuscript.

Folio N° 3.
80th Field Co RE

Place	Date	Hour	Summary of Events and Information	Remarks and references to Appendices
NAOURS	Feb 1st	18th	Work as before & Build Baths Supply and Horse standings at villages of NAOURS, WARGNIES & TALMAS : WARGNIES	
	10	22nd	ditto.	
	22nd	1st 29th	Summary of Works done during month. 7th - 29th by 80th Field Co. less 1 Section	
			Horse Standings	
			6100 sq feet 9" chalk foundations with 3" cinders on surface - WARGNIES	
			3250 " " " " " " " - NAOURS	
			Baths. Includes cleaning out barns, general repair and white-wash	
			- approx accommodation - 2300 men - WARGNIES	
			57 baths " " 2200 " - TALMAS	
			55 " " " 1300 " - NAOURS	
			36 "	
			also fitting doors, repairing windows, fixing latches, and wire bands etc etc.	
			Horse Troughs so far. NAOURS - - 1. 3 Pumps hand for same fitted.	
			WARGNIES - - 1.	
			TALMAS - - 1.	
			Baths. 6 repaired TALMAS. - 1 8" Delivery TANGYE PUMP fitted also 1 8-10 HP	
			3 under repair - TALMAS. Petrol Engine including Engine and Pump house shed	
			Filter. 28 Ablution benches	
			30 Latrines	

B. Blackwell Capt R.E.
O.O. 80th Field Co. R.E.

Army Form C. 2118

WAR DIARY
or
INTELLIGENCE SUMMARY

(Erase heading not required.)

No. 1.
80th Field Co. R.E.

Instructions regarding War Diaries and Intelligence
Summaries are contained in F.S. Regs., Part II.
and the Staff Manual respectively. Title Pages
will be prepared in manuscript.

Place	Date	Hour	Summary of Events and Information	Remarks and references to Appendices
NAOURS	March 1st to 7th		Work continued at last month on Billet Water Supply and horse standings in Villages of NAOURS, TALMAS, WARGNIES and HAVERNAS under C.E. X Corps.	
	8th		The Company left NAOURS and marched to CORBIE. XVIII Division. arrive CORBIE 5.30 p.m. Reported by wire to Majori XVIII Division and await further instructions	
CORBIE	11th		Divisional orders to march to BRAY and join 52nd BRIGADE received Starting 6.10 a.m. Arrived BRAY at 1.30 p.m. with first sections Company moved over in Artillery formation.	
BRAY	12th		Clearing up and fixing Billets and Officers &c. No 4 Section detached	
	13th		Visited Sections to be taken over by This Company with Lieut Brennan for the first time	
	14th		The whole of No 4 Section in dug outs in CARNOY tonight No 4 Section will take over RE work in A, No 2 " " " " A2 No 3 " " " " CARNOY defences CAFFET, LA GUERRE and LAPREE WOODS Scheme BRAY REDUMP, WORKSHOPS &c.	
	15th 16th		No 2 Section moved up to CARNOY Work in A, and A2 and Main communication cutward runs under our Supervision	
	17th		No 3 Section took over No 3 Paraph. waterhed by 202nd R.E	

WAR DIARY

Army Form C. 2118

Place	Date	Hour	Summary of Events and Information	Remarks and references to Appendices
BRAY	18th	—	Company changing Billets with 202 R.E. and taking over their Stores. Reviewing RE Dumps and Workshops.	
	19th	—	CRE 18th Div. inspected N°3 Survey Post with me to see in what state it was handed over. Also inspected sizes of 2" wells run from BRONFAY FARM to CARNOY. These two jobs to be finished by N°3 Section N°2 and to write work in A. and remain. As an M.L. by myself on 14th inst. commenced erection of Gas Engine for BOUTS SAWMILL only the cement bed handed over found to be completed. Much time will be required unfortunately to put Sawmill in decent order. Former Bookkeeper etc in deficit. Shall hand over Divisional Pump (am owner to CRE 18th Bn.)	
	20th	—	Cleaning Billets, digging Latrines. Recroding Cookhouses by N°1 Section and Drivers. Also screening Pontoon Equipment from aerial observations. Erection of Gas Engine. Commencing Workshops. Section 2 and 4 in Trenches. Section 3 Late Supply. N°3 Survey and Navi Communication for A. and AL. (CARNOY, SHEFFIELD and PERONNE AVENUES)	
	21st to 31st	—	All as above. Summary overleaf done overleaf.	

Army Form C. 2118

WAR DIARY
or
INTELLIGENCE SUMMARY
(Erase heading not required.)

80th Field Coy.

folio 2

Place	Date	Hour	Summary of Events and Information	Remarks and references to Appendices

Summary of work done during month of March 1916

No 4 Section.

3   Dugout completed in CAPPET WOOD
    BRICK ALLEY
1   Steel shelters left uncompleted by 202 Co. completed BRICK ALLEY.
1   Officers Room Dug out) completed in BRICK ALLEY.
1   Dressing Room Dug out)
1   Old trench dug out repaired. A 9/6
2   Parapet shelters erected in front line (3 complete)
7   Spindle proof shelters erected in trench just off front line

"   Reconnaissance for front line made and necessary materials
    sent up to forward dumps in front line
7   Removal of Railway 50' in front of A 9/4 and 50' behind to
    prevent enemy tapping messages from our forward telephone
    (This work in hand.)

1   Repair of WELL and WINDLASS in CARNOY fixing hand pump
    and laying 180 yards 1½" Main Completed.
12 Repair to CARNOY PARKWAY of required between A 9/4 and CARNOY.

"   Also C.E. H.Q. Dug out in COKE AVENUE
    R.E. H.Q. " " CUMBERLAND AVENUE) in hand.

WAR DIARY or INTELLIGENCE SUMMARY

Army Form C. 2118

folio 4.

80th Field Coy RE

Place	Date	Hour	Summary of Events and Information	Remarks and references to Appendices

Resumé of work done during month (contd.)

No. 2 Section
Priming BERWICK AVENUE
2 Dug out completed in BRICK ALLEY
Repairs to Trench dug out in Centre Section of Sector
4 Splinter Proof Shelters in hand just off front line. (1 complete.)
6 Parapet Shelters in front line.
1 Steel Dug out for STOKES gun crews.
1 Dug out for 2" Mortar Battery
1 Repair of Dug out in CARPET WOOD in hand
1 Opening up MERCHISTON AVENUE
3 Instruction of Infantry parties in rapid wiring

No. 3 Section
Water Supply
125 yards 4" Main laid
"   " 2"   "   "
Erecting 3 1800 Tanks at CONTOUR WOOD in hand } between BRONFAY FARM and PERONNE AV
Cleaning 1 and fixing SHEFFIELD AVENUE, CARNOY AVENUE, and PERONNE AVENUE in hand
No. 4 Army post in hand newly completed (fifteen ones from 52 RE)

Army Form C. 2118

WAR DIARY
or
INTELLIGENCE SUMMARY
(Erase heading not required.)

folio 5   80th Field Coy R.E.

Place	Date	Hour	Summary of Events and Information	Remarks and references to Appendices

No 1 Section in BRAY.

Section of 5 Armoury huts.
1 Band Stand
1 Company Office

Organizing, equipt arranging XVIII DIV. R.E. Dump, roads & same for about 50" made was handed over to CRE XVIII DIV.

Erection of { PETROL ENGINE
{ SAWBENCH
{ BANDSAW.
{ WORKSHOP

Erection of new { COOKHOUSES } To supply 57th Bde and running same
{ LATRINES } for 80th R.E.
{ INCINERATORS }

Arranging and lighting billets taken over from 202 R.E.
Running Plant at BRAY BATHS
BRAY WELL
SUZANNE PUMPING STATION.

Repair to CORBIE - BRAY - ROAD - road collapsed (opening crater about 15 feet in DIAM 13 feet deep) into underground passages. Bridged over by crib pier and 8" timber frames. Top nailed and concrete.

B. Schomberg
Capt RE

WAR DIARY
or
INTELLIGENCE SUMMARY

Army Form C. 2118

8th Australian FE
Vol 10

September. Folio 1.

Place	Date	Hour	Summary of Events and Information	Remarks and references to Appendices
LA THIEULOYE	1/9/16		Training. Entrenching digging & rapid wiring. Attended exhibition of Flammenwerfer	WMcCartie
	2/9/16		Training. Defence of woods BOIS CARNOYE.	
	3/9/16		Training. Company battle.	
	4/9/16		Training.	
	5/9/16		Training.	
	6/9/16		Training.	
	7/9/16		Training.	
	8/9/16		Training.	
	9/9/16		Company moved to NEUVILLE AU CORNET.	
	10/9/16		Company moved to BEAUDRICOURT	
	11/9/16		Company moved to RAINCHEVEL	
	12/9/16		Training	
	13/9/16		Training	
	14/9/16		Training	
	15/9/16		Training	
	16/9/16		Training	
	17/9/16		Training	

WAR DIARY
or
INTELLIGENCE SUMMARY

Army Form C. 2118

Aug 1916 Folio 2

Place	Date	Hour	Summary of Events and Information	Remarks and references to Appendices
Rue Marle	8/8/16		Continued work on Reserve line in front of BATT. H.Q. & behind DEAD COW FARM. Revetting front line in SALIENT. Wing Trenches in Right locality & repairing support line on the Left. Continued work in Left Sub Section.	
"	9/8/16		On Right Sub Section as yesterday 8/8/16. & Repairing RUE DE BOIS & Revetting WILLOW AVENUE. Revetting & Repairing Right flank of CHARDS FARM SALIENT & MINERS LANE. Tunnelling under LILLE ROAD front line. Shortening parapet, building fire step & traverse. COWGATE AVENUE. BRICK STEET.	
"	10/8/16		Same as 9/8/16 & repaired trucks & rails of front line tramway. Completed roof on Machine Gun H.E. Shelter. Wiring revetting frames in flanking breastwork & No. SALOP AVENUE.	
"	11/8/16		Right Subsector same as 9/8/16. Left Subsector same as 9/8/16 & laying new tram rails on L.5 road behind SUBSIDIARY LINE Left of CHARDS FARM. MUNNERY LANE. Repairing pump engine.	
"	12/8/16		Right Subsector same as 9/8/16. Left Subsector same as 11/8/16.	
"	13/8/16		No 3 Section training. No 2 Section carried on Right Subsector work as on 9/8/16 Left Subsector continued work on tram rails, tunnelling under LILLE ROAD revetting MINERS LANE & flanking bay 66 - 65. No 4 Section training	
"	14/8/16		No 2 Section training. No 3 Section carried on Right Subsector work as on 9/5/16. Part of Company had baths, filled in shell holes, RUE MARLE.	

WAR DIARY
or
INTELLIGENCE SUMMARY

Army Form C. 2118

Instructions regarding War Diaries and Intelligence Summaries are contained in F.S. Regs., Part II and the Staff Manual respectively. Title Pages will be prepared in manuscript.

(Erase heading not required.)

Place	Date	Hour	Summary of Events and Information	Remarks and references to Appendices
RAINCHEVAL	18/7/0	—	Training of officers N.C.Os recently in Rainch area.	
	19/7/0		Training	
	20/7/0		Training — laying out practice trenches for infantry attack men.	
LEALVILLERS	21/5/0		Move to LEALVILLERS	
MARTINSAART	22/9/0	—	MARTINSAART — Transport at LEALVILLERS	
	23/7/0		Company under Lt Dawes cleared LEMBURG TRENCH. Remaining officers reconnoitred position Lt Knight	Villa of 1/8/16
			INGLASS not THIEPVAL WOOD Johnson post communication roads/trenches.	
			Remainder officers reconnoitred THIEPVAL AVENUE CAMPBELL AVENUE - Russian Sap, AUTHUILLE line of communication further held by the 49th Div. — PRINCES STREET	
			TOLD GERMAN front line and position for assembly trench.	
			At night the front or 1st Assembly Trench was taped out — (New Trench) by 2 whips of East Surreys the 2nd Assembly Trench by already by & feet was dug deeper. 100	
			The 3rd Assembly was taped out 50 by 2 pioniers of 49th Division.	
			150	
			Old Bock Trench line was dug out by pioniers of 49th Division. Jun 145 to 84 66 a communication	
			trench from OB Lt to 87 Infantry Assembly trench was cut by East Surreys.	
			Much time was wasted because the enemy put 5/9" High Division failed	
			to arrive and eventually the works taped out without a covering party. and the covering party was laid up and patrolling to tape line by the cav—	

1875 Wt. W593/826 1,000,000 4/15 J.B.C. & A. A.D.S.S./Forms/C. 2118.

WAR DIARY or INTELLIGENCE SUMMARY

Army Form C. 2118

Place	Date	Hour	Summary of Events and Information	Remarks and references to Appendices
MARTINSART	24/11		**No 3 section** started preparing dump in old trench further up & pt 75 and clearing out & tidying up comm. trench running parallel to Aveluy L. of C. from Krilch to Bose wit. his cmpt. to 42.	Killed Cpl. H.S.
			An. type At night this section put in 25clips of 186 mm of Pennis 182, 45 Bruns in to Bose wt. line. This further was thus supmd to find communication trench up to points on 1st Assembly trench.	
			No 2 section Repaired tramlines a/ PRINCES AVENUE and commenced repairs pipe line & Johnsons Post.	
			No 4 section Supmd. the S. H². for M.G.W.L. [illegible] Regt on 3rd Assembly Trench a/point 72 and putin 25 cliffs of [illegible] dump on S.K.1 pt. 75 & Assembly Trench and a party of 25 Lanc. Fusilier Pioneers off 45 to dug in the II nd Assembly Trench & finish ten falle off a communication trench was also dug out where head of PRINCES STREET at pt 403 up to 1st Assembly Trench on the same line as the line of Apple trees.	

WAR DIARY or INTELLIGENCE SUMMARY

Army Form C. 2118

Place	Date	Hour	Summary of Events and Information	Remarks and references to Appendices
MARTINSART	25th		No 1 Section - Erected notice boards and map location numbers at junctions of trenches throughout into maps 57d SE. - Bottoming out the III—rd Assembly trench by day. Brought panorama of the Leuwe iof.part.II. – trenches out to IIIrd Assembly trench.	Pulleon of Maps
			No 2 Section - Formed a sump at Johnsons post into aid of Cny Queens 1 Cny of Bedfords. (This sump was destroyed by shell fire later in the day).	
			No 3 Section Continued forming sumps at pt 53 - Old Boch front line with 1Cny Queens & 1Cny Beds. Also finished off the communication trench running parallel to Russian Sap + from pt 42 as noted overleaf -	
			No 4 Section Finishing off B.H.Q. Dugout at pt 72 and worked on Newly formed trench W.N.W. at night. Relief of Queens and Norths	
MARTINSART	June 22nd - 25th		The Coy was continually employed in finding guides in addition to engineering work. It is of great advantage knowing the cny in advance of the infantry as they get to know the trenches and are of immense assistance in assembling troops	

WAR DIARY
or
INTELLIGENCE SUMMARY

Army Form C. 2118

Place	Date	Hour	Summary of Events and Information	Remarks and references to Appendices
Martinsart	26th		Sections were assembled according to orders copy of which are attached.	
		6:30 pm	It was apparent that the 54th Inf Bde had not passed beyond 2nd objective. Orders were reported	
		6.34 pm	Orders issued to No II & IV sections to return to Martinsart, & to No I & III sections to proceed to Chateau Thiepval. OC proceeded to Chateau via Russian Sap — started the 2 sections off to the Chateau & preceded them.	H. Moorcroft Lt
		7.45 pm	Arrival at Chateau Thiepval. It was found that the line ran roughly with trench from R25b62 – R25b40 – R25d08. Having consulted OC Middlesex it was decided that No II & VIII sections were both employed in carrying water & bomb ammunition. Plans set to Chateau Thiepval & during the night these 2 sections made two journeys from Chateau Thiepval & Paisley Dump Avenue "m" Dump at junction of Inskilling Av & Paisley Av carrying ammunition to the Chateau.	
			Three attempts were impossible to do any engineering work as the line was far from firmly established and the real pressing need was ammunition. An attempt line at Russian Sap front line near Maison Grise. Casualties: Sapper Brown wounded, Sapper Scantly in arm from line near Maison Grise.	

WAR DIARY

Place	Date	hour	Summary of events & information	Remarks
Martinsart	27th	8 a.m.	No 4 section started from MARTINSART to consolidate pt 143 on the 2nd objective at THIEPVAL. Remained in Reserve till dark when they proceeded to pt 143	All these Capts.
			No 2 section also left MARTINSART to follow on Russian Sap. avoiding attack on the Schwaben redoubt.	
			No 1 & 3 not being	
	28th	1.30 pm	No 1 section 10th men from no 4 section at pt 143.	
		3 pm	No 2 section moved to pt 49 on Schwaben Redoubt, junction of MARKET GRABEN and sea German Support line and commenced a strong point with 2 platoons of West Kent Regiment.	
			Later they moved to point 22 and point 45 and cleared trenches of the bomb stops at these places.	
	29th	7 am	No 3 section relieved No 2 section at pt 22. Casualties on the way up	Sheidenger, Sgr Brooks, Sgr Home, Bellew.
			The No 2 section wearily able to tackle pt 22 as pt 45 had been lost.	Rutter, Stanley, L/Cpl Q Gallop, Sketch.
	30th		No 4 section relieved no 1 section at pt 143. No 3 of THIEPVAL. Sappers further wounded.	
			No 1 & 4 section at work in relief in pt 143. N edge of THIEPVAL and at well	THIEPVAL pt 67
			No 2 & 3 sections at work on pt 22 — Work on point 145 impossible.	

Vol 11
Army Form C2118

WAR DIARY October 1916

Summary of Events and Information   Folio 1

Place	Date	Hour		Remarks
MARTINSART	1st		No 2&3 section working in relief in P.22 - cleared hitherto to point 45 mtr Platoon of BERKSHIRE Regt - Shaft run for M.G. at pt 13. 1 other Mummy wounded by shell Sgt Pelham wounded. No 1 & 4 section working in points 15 & 27.	Sgt Rifle wounded
	2nd		do. do.	
	3rd		Handed over to 92nd Coy.	
			No 4 section worked at Lancashire Dump erecting shelters	
			No 3 section pipe line	
			No 2 section cleared Dugout for 92nd Coy in IMPERVAL	
			No 4 section reconnoitring position of pole targets	
			No 1 section Lancashire Dump erecting shelters	
	4th		No 2 section making pole targets	
			No 4 " reconnoitre to position of pole targets	
			No 3 section making pole targets	

Army Form C. 2118.

WAR DIARY
or
INTELLIGENCE SUMMARY

(Erase heading not required.)

October 1916 Folio 2

Place	Date	Hour	Summary of Events and Information	Remarks and references to Appendices
MARTINSART	5/10/16		Company moved to HEDAUVILLE into bivouacs.	
HEDAUVILLE	6/10/16		Dismounted portion of Company marched to ACHEUX, entrained for CANDAS & marched (to billets) at ÉPECAMPS. Mounted section moved by road to billets at RAINCHEVAL	
ÉPECAMPS & RAINCHEVAL	7/10/16		Dismounted portion of Company repairing billets. Mounted Section moved by road to billets at ÉPECAMPS.	
ÉPECAMPS	8/10/16		Musketry & making horse standings	
"	9/10/16		Repairing billets. Company based at BERNAVILLE.	
"	10/10/16		Drill, musketry & making horse standings	
"	11/10/16		" " "	
"	12/10/16		" " "	
"	13/10/16		" " " & repairing wells at BERNEVILLE	
"	14/10/16		" " " "	
"	15/10/16		" " " "	
BEAUVAL	16/10/16		Company marched to BEAUVAL.	
CONTAY	17/10/16		Company marched to CONTAY	
BOUZINCOURT	18/10/16		Company marched to BOUZINCOURT.	
"	19/10/16		Company marched to OVILLERS-LA-BOISELLE. No 4 Section & transport lines USNA HILL.	
OVILLERS LA BOISELLE & USNA HILL	20/10/16		Clearing dug outs & making notice boards.	

WAR DIARY or INTELLIGENCE SUMMARY

(Erase heading not required.)

October 1916. Folio 3.

Place	Date	Hour	Summary of Events and Information	Remarks and references to Appendices
OVILLERS LA BOISELLE & USNA HILL	21/10/16		Preparing Bde. H.Q. dugout at R.29.d.o.8. Commenced Bn. H.Q. dugout at R.24.a.3.2. Making sign boards.	
	22/10/16		As for 21/10/16. Commenced Bn. H.Q. dugout at 23 Central. Also commenced dugout Collecting Station at R.29.d.o.8.	
	23/10/16		As for 22/10/16. Completed Bn. H.Q. dugout. Erected trench notice boards.	
”	24/10/16		As for 23/10/16. New Bn. H.Q.	
	25/10/16		As for 24/16. plus work on shelter trenches for 2.R.E. section at R.29.d.o.7.9 making new roads at dump.	
”	26/10/16		As for 25/16. plus cleaning dugouts at top of CENTRE WAY IN	
	27/10/16		As for 26/16. plus constructing dugouts in REGINA TRENCH. carrying forward dumps & making frames & options.	
”	28/10/16		As for 27/16.	
	29/10/16		As for 28/16. plus Repairing tramway POZIERES to R.29 Central. making infantry track from POZIERES to CENTRE WAY IN. Repairing dugouts next CENTRE WAY IN in ZOLLERN TRENCH.	
”	30/10/16		As for 29/16 plus constructing new Bn. H.Q GRANDCOURT ROAD & grubbing track POZIERES to CENTRE WAY IN.	
	31/10/16		As for 30/16 plus clearing SUDBURY TRENCH. Sapper F. Johnson wounded.	

Army Form C. 2118.

80 2/A Coy R.E.

WAR DIARY or INTELLIGENCE SUMMARY

(Erase heading not required.)

November 1916.   Folio. 1.

Place	Date	Hour	Summary of Events and Information	Remarks and references to Appendices
OVILLERS LA BOISELLE OUSNA HILL	1/11/16	80th Rue Coy R.E.	Clearing & repairing dugouts in CENTRE WAY IN. Enlarging dugouts in ZOLLERN TRENCH. Making Signboards.	
	2/11/16		As for 1/11/16. Pte Webb on exhibition for wounded at R.29 Central. Spr 3754 3 Sapper Ballantine killed.	
	3/11/16		As for 2/11/16	
	4/11/16		As for 3/11/16 plus erecting screen across valley N of McDONNELL RD & fitting up Bn HQ POZIERES	
	5/11/16		As for 4/11/16 plus cleaning SUDBURY TRENCH & widening KENORA TRENCH.	
	6/11/16		Same as 5/11/16 less across McDONNELL RD. Plus making man hole. I.L.D. housemen unit.	
	7/11/16		Finishing collecting station near R.29 Central, making ramp between GRANDCOURT ROAD & sunken track behind screen N of McDONNELL TR. Work on dugouts R.29 Central & CENTRE WAY IN. Making mining case & board walk at POZIERES DUMP	
	8/11/16		Making mining cases POZIERES DUMP continued. Cook house & coffee bar GRANDCOURT ROAD. Repairing CENTRE WAY IN & SUDBURY.	
	9/11/16		Cleaning out CENTRE WAY & SUDBURY Trenches out as at 8/11/16. Lieut R.Y.S. Downs & Sapper Wentworth 576440 Wounded. (been shell).	
	10/11/16		No 2 Section battled. Cleaning communication trenches & making mining frames, dog kennels & board walk.	
	11/11/16		Work on dugouts VANCOUVER TRENCH, cleaning CENTRE WAY & SUDBURY, making mining frames & duckboard walks	
	12/11/16		As for 11/11/16 + enlarging Bn H.Q. CLIFF TRENCH.	

WAR DIARY or INTELLIGENCE SUMMARY

Army Form C. 2118.

Folio 2.

Place	Date	Hour	Summary of Events and Information	Remarks and references to Appendices
	13/11/16		Clearing KENDRA TRENCH. Making mining frames & mats. Dugouts CLIFF TRENCH. VANCOUVER TRENCH.	
	14/11/16		No 4 Section bathed. Work on for 13/11/16	
	15/11/16		Making mining cars & mats into man loads. Splinter proofs of R 29 Central. Repairing dugouts OVILLERS	
	16/11/16		Making mining frames. Dugouts VANCOUVER & GRANDCOURT Trenches. Making man loads.	
	17/11/16		Moving Div. dump from POZIERES to TULLOCH'S CORNER. Cut out FIELD TRENCH. Work on huts at D.H.Q. Clearing out dugouts OVILLERS. No 4541 Sapper TK Rt wounded H2544 2nd Cpl Penson "	
	18/11/16		Work on dugouts OVILLERS & huts at D.H.Q.	
	19/11/16		Work on LANCASHIRE TRENCH. laying mat walk to DESIRE TRENCH. New trenches at OVILLERS, huts at D.H.Q. & work on dump.	
	20/11/16		Work on LANCASHIRE TRENCH & mine shafts in HESSIAN TRENCH. mat walk to within 200 yds of DESIRE TRENCH. Work at dump & huts at D.H.Q. & OVILLERS.	
	21/11/16		Work on Dump, dugouts in HESSIAN TRENCH & Nissen bow huts	
	22/11/16		As for 21/11/16 plus laying mat walk from REGINA to DESIRE TRENCH & grid walk from RIFLE DUMP to LANCASHIRE TRENCH & dugouts ZOLLERN TRENCH.	
	23/11/16		As for 22/11/16.	
	24/11/16		1 Section working at Dump. 2 Section on dugouts in ZOLLERN & HESSIAN TRENCHES. 1 Section on huts at OVILLERS.	

WAR DIARY
or
INTELLIGENCE SUMMARY

(Erase heading not required.)

Army Form C. 2118.

Folio 3.

Place	Date	Hour	Summary of Events and Information	Remarks and references to Appendices
	25/11/16		As for 24th.	
	26/11/16		Company bathed.	
	27/11/16		Quiet.	
	28/11/16		Improving accommodation at OVILLERS.	
	29/11/16			
	30/11/16			

M MacCampbell Capt
O.C. 98th Coy R.E.

Army Form C. 2118.

WAR DIARY
or
INTELLIGENCE SUMMARY

(Erase heading not required.)

8th Yorks
December 1916.   Folio 1.

Place	Date	Hour	Summary of Events and Information	Remarks and references to Appendices
OVILLERS LA BOISELLE	1/12/16		Making horse standings, clearing trenches OVILLERS. making mining frames.	
	2/12/16		Same as for 1st	
	3/12/16		Same as for 1st	
	4/12/16		Work on dugouts & M.G. emplacements ZOLLERN TRENCH. making mining frames.	
	5/12/16		Same as for 4/12	
	6/12/16		Same as 4/12/16	
	7/12/16		Same as 4/12/16	
	8/12/16		Same as 4/12/16	
	9/12/16		Same as 4/12/16	
	10/12/16		Same as 4/12/16 Blackmare L.D. R.E.2 26 evacuated	
	11/12/16		Same as 4/12/16	
	12/12/16		Same as 4/12/16	
	13/12/16		Same as 4/12/16	
	14/12/16		Same as 4/12/16	
	15/12/16		Same as 4/12/16	
	16/12/16		Same as 4/12/16	
	17/12/16		Same as 4/12/16	
	18/12/16		Same as 4/12/16 Sapper Deane O.J. Wounded	
	19/12/16		Same as 4/12/16	

Army Form C. 2118.

WAR DIARY
or
INTELLIGENCE SUMMARY

(Erase heading not required.)

Folio. 2.

Place	Date	Hour	Summary of Events and Information	Remarks and references to Appendices
PUCHIEVILLERS.	20/12/16		Backing wagons & preparing for move to ABBEVILLE area. Mounted portion moved to	
	21/12/16		Dismounted portion of Company entrained at ALBERT. Dismounted portion of Company moved to BEAUMETZ.	
	22/12/16		Dismounted portion of Company detrained at ST RIQUIER & marched to HUETTEN-OUVILLE. Mounted portion of Company marched to OUVILLE.	
	23/12/16		Work improving billets & horse lines.	
	24/12/16		Same as for 23/12.	
	25/12/16		Christmas Day. Rest.	
	26/12/16		Same as for 23/12.	
	27/12/16		Nos 1 & 2 Sections training with 54th Bde. Nos 4 Sect. moved to CANCHY. Nos 1 & 3 Sections improving billets & horse standings.	
	28/12/16		No 4 Section improving billets at CANCHY. No 2 Sect. moved to DRUCAT. Nos 1 & 3 Sections improving billets & making horse standings.	
	29/12/16		No 4 Section improving billeting accommodation at CANCHY.	
			No 2 Section " " " DRUCAT.	
			Nos 1 & 3 Sections " billets & horse standings OUVILLE.	
	30/12/16		Same as 29/12.	
	31/12/16		Same as 30/12.	

M. Power
Capt.
O.C. 11 Field Coy N.Z.

WAR DIARY
or
INTELLIGENCE SUMMARY

Army Form C. 2118.

80 Fd Coy R.E.

January 1917.

Place	Date	Hour	Summary of Events and Information	Remarks and references to Appendices
OUVILLE CHATEAU, OUVILLE.	1/1/17		Resting:- Lieut. McFarlane with 2 N.C.O.s and 6 Sappers proceeded to St. RIQUIER for work in 1st Army Bridging School.	
ARSEVILLE AREA	2/1/17		Work proceeded in the various areas:- Nos. 1 & 3 Sections at OUVILLE CAV. worked on Divisional School at ABBEY on Divisional Rifle Range near NEUILLY l'HÔPITAL and on the Company's billets in OUVILLE CHATEAU. No. 2 Section worked in the DOMVAST AREA and was billeted in DOMVAST No. 4 — — — CANCHY AREA — — — CANCHY. The work mainly consisted in :- In carrying the accommodation in the villages by the erection of Nissen huts — in erection of incinerators, cook-houses, cart-horse-wash-man, public latrines, and horse-standings; In improving and repairing existing buildings; and putting up carters, shelters, screens, access roads.	

WAR DIARY
or
INTELLIGENCE SUMMARY

Army Form C. 2118.

Place	Date	Hour	Summary of Events and Information	Remarks and references to Appendices
OUVILLE.	3/1/17		Work on above for 2/1/17. — Sapper O'Sullivan sent to Hospital Sick	
	4/1/17		do.	
	5/1/17		do.	
	6/1/17		do. 146452 Spr Williams } Sent to Hospital Sick 6.1.17 59100 Spr Mitchell }	
	7/1/17		do.	
	8/1/17		Nos. 2 & 4 Sections rejoined the Company at OUVILLE CHATEAU from DRUCAT and CANCHY respectively.	
	9/1/17		Spent in billets collecting equipment, cleaning wagons &c. Afternoon spent resting. Lt. Grant, 31st Divisional Engineer, was shewn work in progress in DRUCAT and CANCHY area.	

WAR DIARY or INTELLIGENCE SUMMARY

Army Form C. 2118.

(Erase heading not required.)

Place	Date	Hour	Summary of Events and Information	Remarks and references to Appendices
OUVILLE	10/7/17		Spent in billets preparing for move.	
FRANSU	11/7/17		Moved to FRANSU.	
GORGES	12/7/17		Moved to GORGES. - (61500 Gpr Weir to hospital. Still evacuating on the march)	
	13/7/17		At GORGES. Kit inspection and football.	
VAL de MAISON	14/7/17		Moved to VAL de MAISON.	
MARTINSART	15/7/17		Moved to MIDLAND HUTS about V.9.b.8.0. South of MARTINSART.	
X.2.a.2.2.	16/7/17		Disposition of Company:- Coy. Headquarters & one German trench and two roads in dug-outs about X.2.a.2.2. Nos. 1 & 3 Sections in dug-outs about R.28.c.8.6. Nos. 2 & 4 Section in dug-outs MOUQUET FARM R.33.b.2.9. Divisional and mounted orderlies and Q.M. stores at MIDLAND HUTS about V.9.b.8.0.	
	17/7/17		Officers and N.C.O.s reconnoitring divisional forward area. Improving dug-outs.	

Army Form C. 2118.

WAR DIARY
or
INTELLIGENCE SUMMARY
(Erase heading not required.)

Instructions regarding War Diaries and Intelligence Summaries are contained in F. S. Regs., Part II. and the Staff Manual respectively. Title Pages will be prepared in manuscript.

Place	Date	Hour	Summary of Events and Information	Remarks and references to Appendices
X.20.7.2.	18/1/17		As above for 17th.	
	19/1/17		Started forming dumps in battalion sector. Training and (Infantry) accommodation in dugouts at H.Q. and others including Refreshment outpost, (Regt Aid Station.) Also making good the excavations of dug outs in HESSIAN TRENCH and clearing entrances connecting Main gorge in dug outs STUFF REDOUBT and at MOUQUET FARM. Firing up Brigade Headquarters X.20.2.3.	Sr. Scott / Bar & Hope 17th Sr. Scott / Ego Gregor including (Regt. Batt.Sd.Bn) Sr. Major / Lieut. Stopford Sr. Stothart 17th
	20th		As above also clearing and resettling HESSIAN and ZOLLERN TRENCHES. Making wiring entries into no man's land to enemy's front line — DESIRE TRENCH.	
	21/1/17		As above. All digging has become exceedingly difficult owing to very hard frost; carrying materials has also become difficult especially at night owing to frost making ground uneven as always. Enclosing dugouts at R.33.b.7.3.	
	22/1/17		As above. Work of Sanitation and reconstruction, and recloaking is carried on according to Divisional and Brigade Instructions and Programme.	Sr. Lawler, D./ Hospital Sick Sr. Beath. J. 22.1.17

WAR DIARY
or
INTELLIGENCE SUMMARY

Army Form C. 2118.

(Erase heading not required.)

Place	Date	Hour	Summary of Events and Information	Remarks and references to Appendices
Con. Alb. X.2.a.2.2.	23/1/17		Carried on with erection of dugout sheds R.33.b.7.3.	
			Repairing duckboards Mouquet Farm R.33.d.3.8.	
			Stuff Redoubt R.21.c.6.5.	
			Regina Trench R.22.a.2.7.	
			Repairing and relaying trench tracks to Stuff Redoubt, R.21.c.	
			Clearing and widening trenches Regina Trench R.21.a.5.5. and R.22.c.2.7.	
			Hessian Trench R.21.d.5.7.	
			Zollern Trench R.21.b.4.9. to R.22.b.4.5.	
			Began new track from Regina to dugouts in Fabeck R.22.b.4.5.	
			Forming dumps at Gravel Pit R.27.c.3.3. and Rifle Dump R.28.c.6.2.	
			and preparing materials & mining material.	
	24/1/17		No workable parties available. Sappers carried on when possible. Sapper Garrod W. } Sent to Hospital 24/1/17 Spr Calvert J. }	
	25/1/17		Handed over left sub sector - from Sixteen Road to left. - to 79th Field Co. R.E. 7.6.5. 2nd Lt. Aitken. Our left down to Coy H.Q. X.2.a.2.2.	

Army Form C. 2118.

WAR DIARY
or
INTELLIGENCE SUMMARY

(Erase heading not required.)

Place	Date	Hour	Summary of Events and Information	Remarks and references to Appendices
Coy HQ X.29.2.2.	26/17		Repairing various dugouts in FABECK TRENCH. ZOLLERN TRENCH HESSIAN TRENCH and at RIFLE DUMP. Opening up and clearing REGINA TRENCH R.22.6.8.2. ZOLLERN TRENCH R.28.b.4.9. Making platform for return at TULLOCH'S DOME R.33.d.5.2. Improving various billets. C.J. H/s. C.M. explain above for clearing REGINA TR. between W. MIRAUMONT Road and SIXTEEN Road being supplied Brigade as working party. Commenced organising dumps approaches to for this. Permanent finishing party attached to Company for funking materials from DILLEN'S to GRANDS Pit. of 2 platoons.	
	27/17		No working parties into the Brigade relief in line. Sgt. Jellings A. sent to Hosp. injured owing to fall Clearing and revetting ZOLLERN TRENCH Commenced work on new advanced dressing Station R.33.d.2.9. Divided REGINA TRENCH into sectors and sub sectors; renumbered rub/s to various sectors; and preparing our new route for right relief sector. Infantry Brigade and by Kadogan Gd., West Road.	

2449 Wt. W14957/Mgo 750,000 1/16 J.B.C. &A. Forms/C.2118/12.

WAR DIARY or INTELLIGENCE SUMMARY

Army Form C. 2118.

Place	Date	Hour	Summary of Events and Information	Remarks and references to Appendices
Coy. Hrs. X.2.a.2.	28th.		Carried on as above. Matters work in Nulla CRUCIFIX CORNER W.11.d.9.1. do. do. Advanced Dressing Station, R.33.d.2.9. Carried on Calais Multi-at-Advanced Dressing Station, HUN TANK R.33.d.0.0.(about). Work on REGINA TR. which was to have started night 29/h cancelled by C.R.E. tonight on account of front.	
	29th.		Preparing REGINA TRENCH for dugouts. Obtaining and supervising arrangements for large dugouts and dugouts in REGINA TR. Repairing (men neither HESSIAN TR. R.22.d.2.8. to junction of WIGAN LANE with HESSIAN TR. R.22.d.7.9. Meeting Maser for Hurls at WARWICK HUTS (about X.I.c.) on North side of NAB Rd. do. do. Multi-burrow CRUCIFIX CORNER W.11.d.9.1. Clearing dugouts RIFLE DUMP for TRAMS. Advance front. Excavating for shelter to Advanced Dressing Station R.33.d.2.9. Fixing up Dressing Station (Calais Multi.) at HUN TANK.	

WAR DIARY or INTELLIGENCE SUMMARY

Army Form C. 2118.

Place	Date	Hour	Summary of Events and Information	Remarks and references to Appendices
X.2.a.2.2. Coy HQ.	30/1/17		As for 29/1/17. Started mining in REGINA TRENCH.	2 O/r Leonard W. sent to Hospital 30.1.17
	31/1/17		As for 30th. Also repairing tracks at OVILLERS DUMP and repairing entrance at dug-out ZOLLERN TRENCH.	Spr McLeod Scott. Hospital 31.1.17

Munro.
Capt.
O.C. 61 Field Coy. R.E.
1/2/17.

WAR DIARY or INTELLIGENCE SUMMARY

Army Form C. 2118.

80 Field Coy R.E.

No. 5

Place	Date	Hour	Summary of Events and Information Feb. 1917 John 1	Remarks and references to Appendices
Coy HRs K.20.a.2.2.	4/2/17		For work on Roads and Progress see APPENDIX A. 2 additional permanent platoons allotted for work from 52nd Div. This makes 4 platoons in all for the Company i.e. one per section.	A.
	7/2/17		45696 Spr Hulbert sent to hospital. 3/4/17 46161 Spr McIntyre J. sent to hospital. Suffering from a fall.	
	8/2/17		Work in two interrupted most. Commencement of period of active operations by the pioneers in the line. No working parties available for Brigade & Divs Nos. 1. 3. and 4. Section Rested. For work on Roads and Progress see APPENDIX B.	B.
	14/2/17		Preliminary instructions for Operations issued; see APPENDIX C.	C.

WAR DIARY
INTELLIGENCE SUMMARY

Summary of Events and Information Feb. 1917 No 2

Place	Date	Hour	Summary of Events and Information	Remarks and references to Appendices
Coy. Hqrs. X.2.a.2.2.	16/2/17		For work in hand and progress see APPENDIX D. Operation orders issued; see APPENDIX E.	D. E.
	17/2/17	9 a.m.	Maj. Hart S.T.D.S.E. exhibit 3A. O.C. issued orders for Tunnels Attn. Offrs. (54th Inf. Bde.) R.23.c.8.5. Lt. Field O.C. No 4 Coy. K proceed with his section and attached infantry to consolidate strong point No 5. This strong point was completed (with a double line of French concertina wire) about 4.30 p.m.; and was taken over and garrisoned by the 11th Royal Fusiliers then.	
		2.40 p.m.	G.O.C. 54th Inf. Bde. informed O.C. that the enemy Robert Kn.a and b. had been taken and that strong points Nos. 1 and 2 (R.11.a.31. and R.11.a.92.) [illegible] heights.	

WAR DIARY or INTELLIGENCE SUMMARY

Summary of Events and Information Feb. 1917 Folio 3

Place	Date	Hour	
Cols. Hrs. S2Q22	17/2/17	3.30 p.m.	O.C. went ahead with Lt. Inman, O.C. No.1 Sec., leaving RIFLE DUMP at 3.30 p.m. in order to lay tapes from BOOM RAVINE out to the strong points, and to lay out these strong points. Lt. Mickelum was left to bring forward the two R.E. sections and their two attached infantry platoons to GRANDCOURT TRENCH about R.11.C.5.2., where he was to await further instruction.

O.C. soon found impossible to lay out these strong points, as it was discovered that the enemy were in possession of these points or the ground in their immediate vicinity. Lt. Inman and the O.C. managed to reach the position of point No.2., but later, Lt. Inman and Sapper Islant were killed by M.G. fire while laying out this position. The enemy post must have been evidence of a sniper who escaped from the position of the strong point. |

Army Form C. 2118.

WAR DIARY
or
INTELLIGENCE SUMMARY
(Erase heading not required.)

Instructions regarding War Diaries and Intelligence Summaries are contained in F.S. Regs., Part II. and the Staff Manual respectively. Title Pages will be prepared in manuscript.

Place	Date	Hour	Summary of Events and Information	Remarks and references to Appendices
	17/2/17		Feb 1917 Jebes it. The 65. was frustrated in this attempt to reach the position of Strongpoint No.1 by rifle fire (four or five rifles) from a enemy post on the W. MIRAUMONT RD. at R.11.a.9.2.; he had reached a point about 80 yds. short of the position at R.11.a.9.5. which the enemy appeared to hut along front No.1. No.1 Section and attached infantry of both sections were sent back to dug-outs. No.3 decided perhaps a few of em to that of their Section in the right about R.11.d.0.05.	
	18/2/17		Nos. 1, 2 and 4 Sec. and attached infantry were employed laying and extending the first north from about R.17.c.5.4 towards BEAUCOURT Stan until it reaches 350 yds. of the same by the night 18-19th. No.3 Sec. continued consolidation of captured position and a strong point about R.11.C.55.	

249 Wt. W14957/M90 750,000 1/16. J.B.C. & A. Forms/C.2118/12.

WAR DIARY
or
INTELLIGENCE SUMMARY

(Erase heading not required.)

Instructions regarding War Diaries and Intelligence Summaries are contained in F.S. Regs., Part II. and the Staff Manual respectively. Title Pages will be prepared in manuscript.

Place	Date	Hour	Summary of Events and Information	Remarks and references to Appendices
			Feb 1917 Folio 5	
Coy. HQ. X.2.a.2.	19/2/17.		45740 L/Cpl Gregor W. Wounded in Action 18/2/17 Consolidation & captured position continues. Reconnaissance walk laid following line & Anthony Trench from ZOLLERN TRENCH forward. Field-walk extended further towards BOOM RAVINE. 104433 Spr Grimshaw W. Wounded in Action 19/2/17	
	21/2/17.		Relieved by 9th Lincoln Regt.; both our men killed in the evening. Relief as follows Coy. HQr. Nos. 1, 2 and 3 Secs. above lines	W.9.b.8.5. MIDLAND HUTS Q.2.d.
			No 4 Section in dug-outs	

Army Form C. 2118.

WAR DIARY
or
INTELLIGENCE SUMMARY

(Erase heading not required.)

Instructions regarding War Diaries and Intelligence Summaries are contained in F. S. Regs., Part II. and the Staff Manual respectively. Title Pages will be prepared in manuscript.

Feb 1917 Folio 6

Place	Date	Hour	Summary of Events and Information	Remarks and references to Appendices
Coy HQ. M.G.D.83.	22/2/17		Commenced tooth area work as handed over by 9th Field Coy R.E.	
	23/2/17		No 1 Sec. moved to dugouts Q.24.d.	
			For work in hand and progress see APPENDIX F.	F.
			133486 Spr Jones C. sent to Hospital suffering from Rheumatism	
	28/2/17		For work in hand and progress see APPENDIX G.	G.

M Munro. Capt. R.E.
OC 80th Fd. Coy. R.E.

To CRE 18 Division   Weekly progress report   **APPENDIX A.**

From 80th Fd Coy. RE

Week ending Feb. 3. 1917

Work	Date Commenced	Map Location	Progress	Remarks
Erecting Bath house	27/1/17	Crucifix Corner	50% Completed	
RAMC Shelter	27/1/17	Rifle Dump	Excavation complete for 1 Shelter & 50% of second. Old Gun pit dismantled.	
Advanced Dressing Station	27/1/17	R 33 d 2.9.	Excavation complete for 1 Shelter & 50% Completed for 2 others	
ditto	27/1/17	Hun Tank	Complete with exception of Stretcher racks	
Route for Large Infantry party	27/1/17	L. Regina Trench	Complete. (Maintenance required)	
Dugouts	28/1/17	Regina Trench	Cleared trench for 4 dugouts. Frames in as follows, working from Right 9, 9, 11, 9, 9, 8, 10 & 10,	
Rearranging dumps	28/1/17	O.T dump and Tudor's dump	Completed	
Billets improvements	28/1/17	Coy. H. Qrs.	90% Completed	
Nissen Huts	29/1/17	Warwick Huts	2 Huts 95% Completed to 30/1/17	
Repairing trucks	31/1/17	O.T dump	10 Trucks repaired	
Salvaging	1.2.17	O.T dump	8 Trucks brought in	
Repairing entrance to dugouts	31/1/17	Zollern Trench	80% Complete. Trench required revetting between dugouts	
Revetting	31.1.17	Zollern Tr. from dugout to Wigan Lane	90% Completed	
O.P	2.2.17	Zollern Tr	Work commenced	

3.2.17

J. Munn Capt RE
OC 80 Fd Coy. RE

To CRE 18 Div.   APPENDIX B.
                                            Weekly progress report
From OC 80 Fd Coy RE
                                            Week ending Feb 9. 1917

Work	Date Commenced	Map Location	Progress
Erecting Bath house	27/1/17	Crucifix Corner	Structure complete except floors & fixtures. Sprays &c being fixed
RAMC Shelters	27/1/17	Rifle Dump	Shelter for Stretchers 75% complete. One English shelter 90% complete and excavation for second 80% compl.
Advanced dressing Station	27/1/17	R 33 d 2.9	One English shelter erected, excavation for two others complete
ditto	27.1.17	Hun Tank	Complete
Repairing tracks	3/2/17	OT dump	Tracks completed during week
OP	2/2/17	Zollern Tr:	80% complete
Revetting trench Repairing entrance	3/1/17	Zollern Tr	Repairs to entrance completed. 25 yds cleared & revetted
Tramway Extension	5/2/17	R 34 a 2.7	Formation way completed 230 yds. Rails laid 180 yds. 50 yds rails to lay to join to Rogers Line
Dugouts	28.1.17	REGINA TR	Frames in as follows, working from right 22, 23, 25, 23, 26, 24, 23 & 23. 114 put in during the week

9.2.17

[signature]
Capt RE
OC 80th Fd Coy. RE

APPENDIX C.

Instructions for RE Sections with regard to carrying tools etc.

Tools & RE material

These will be either, ① taken from the respective starting points or, ② drawn from RIRE DUMP or ③ GULLY.

Tools		Where to be drawn
Picks	8. to one per man	②
Shovels	one per man to 12	②
Axes, Felling	1	①
Axes, hand	2	①
Mauls	2	③
Saws, hand	1	①
Crowbar	1	③
Plain Wire	2 small coils	①
Sandbags	10 per man	①
Tracing tapes	10	①
Wire cutters	8. pr	①
Hedging Gloves	8 pr	①
Candles	2 per man	①

Men with only one tool will carry wiring material which will be drawn from the Gully in the following proportions.

2 coils of French Wire
1 coil of Barbed Wire
10 Pickets

Each man must be told exactly what he is to carry and where he is to get it.

The Sections must be organised in squads and worked in squads as far as possible.
It must be firmly impressed on squad commanders that they are responsible for the men in their squads.

Each Section must detail a runner to be at Bde. H.Q. Time to be notified later.

Attached Infantry Platoon

Tools & RE material will be carried as follows:

Tools	Where to be drawn
Picks 8 — 1 per man	(2)
Shovels 1 per man to 12	(2)
Wiring material (in above proportions)	(3)
Sandbags 10 per man	(1)
Candles 1 per man	(1)
Sandbags. 3 lots of 50	(2)

Men with only one tool will carry wiring material or Sandbags

Each man must be told exactly what he is to carry & where he is to get it.

Note:— The dump — RIFLE DUMP — must contain enough picks & shovels so as to allow each man to have one pick & one shovel. The proportion which will be taken on the day will depend on the state of the ground.

Each Section & Platoon must see to the dumping of their tools.

14 . 1 . 17

Munn
OC 80" 70 Coy RE Capt RE

To/ CRE 18th Div

From OC 80th Fd Coy RE

APPENDIX D.
Weekly progress report
Week ending Feb 16 1917

Work	Date Commenced	Map Location	Progress
Erecting Bath house	22/1/17	Crucifix Corner	Ready for use 12/2/17. but not complete. 90% complete
R.A.M.C. Shelters	24/1/17	Rifle Dump	Completed 15/2/17
ditto	27/1/17	R.33 d.2.9	3 Completed 15/2/17
Turning place	10/2/17	R.33 d.2.9	completed
Battle H.Q. for Bde & Battᵉ	1/2/17	R.23 c 8.5.	Completed
Repairing trucks	3/2/17	O T dump	18 trucks repaired
Salvaging ---	3/2/17	---	12 --- Salvaged
Tramway Extension	5/2/17	R.34 a 2.7	Completed
O.P.	7/2/17	ZOLLERN TR	OP completed, 8 beds in dugout. trench to revett
Relaying points	10/2/17	QUARRY LINE	Completed
Ballasting	10/2/17	ROGERS LINE	Completed to RIFLE dump
Mules track	14/2/17	ZOLLERN. TR	Completed
Making bridge	14/2/17	HESSIAN	
Putting a Siding for A.D.P.	15/2/17	THIEPVAL - POZIERS Rd.	Completed
Ramp Shelter	10/2/17	GULLY	Completed
Repairing Grid Walk	15/2/17	FABECK TR. TO SUDBURY TR.	Completed.
Tunnelled dugouts	28/1/17	REGINA TR	Completed.
Battᵉ HQ.	12/2/17	ZOLLERN TR	Completed.

A. Hennessy.
Capt RE
OC 80 Fd Coy. RE

APPENDIX. E.

80th Fd Coy R.E. Orders for 17/2/17.
and Attached Infantry platoons of 54th Inf Bde.

Ref CRE - OO No 1, 54th Bde Preliminary Instructions BM269
and 54th Bde OO No 7.

No 4 Section under 2/Lt Field will parade in fighting
orders, with the unexpended portion of the days ration and
iron rations, at 3.30 a.m. 17/2/17 at Coy. H.Q. X.2.a.2.2

Attached platoons of 11th R Fusiliers, 7th Bedfords and
6th Northants under 2/Lts Roe, Trewman and Hill respectively
will parade in fighting order with the unexpended portion
of the days ration and Iron rations at 3.30 a.m., 17.2.17
at WARWICK HUTS.

All the above will move to their battle locations
which will be as follows:-
(a) No 4 Section & Bedford platoon - dugouts. H.13 and H.14
(b) Fusilier platoon and Northants platoon - dugouts
  H.15 and H.16.
(c) Nos 1 & 3 Sections under 2/Lts Suman & Richardson
  respectively will have their battle location at RIFLE
  DUMP dug outs

All the above to be at Battle locations by 5.00 a.m.
(d) No 2 Sec under Lt Knight will remain at Coy. H.Q.
- X.2.a.2.2.- in reserve.

Middlesex platoon under 2/Lt Anderson will be at
WARWICK HUTS in reserve.

Arrangements as regards tools - where to be
obtained & what to be carried - remain as per
instruction issued 14/2/17

WORK :- No 4 Section under 2/Lt Field, and the attached
  Bedford Platoon will make a strong point at R.11.c.2.5.

No 3 Section under 2/Lt Richardson and the

attached Northants platoon will make a strongpoint at R 11 a 90.

No 1 Section under 2 Lt Inman, and attached Fusilier platoon will make a strong point at R 11 a 3.1.

OC 80th Fd Coy RE, whose H.Qrs will be with Bde at R 23 d.04 will send a message to OC Sections ordering them to move from their locations to commence work on the strong points. Section must pick up M.G's on the way at the bank - R 22 b 9 9.

On completion of Strong points which ought not to take more than 6 hours, a report will be rendered to Brigade direct, who will arrange for the Garrison. The party must man the Strong points until the Garrison arrives, when they will return.

Nos 1 & 3 Section to RIFLE DUMP
Northants & Fusiliers to HESSIAN TRENCH
No 4 Section to Coy. H.Q. x2 a 22.
Bedfords to WARWICK HUTS.

The following runners will be at Bde H.Qrs by 5.30 a.m 17.2.17 and will await instructions there from OC 80th Fd Coy. RE

2 runners — i.e:- one each from No 4 Sec & platoon of Bedfords
2 runners from RIFLE DUMP. i.e: one each from Nos 1 & 3 Section

There also ought to be 2 runners — one from each attached platoon, Northants & Fusiliers — at RE dug out RIFLE DUMP who will carry messages from there to platoons in HESSIAN TRENCH at H 15 & H 16.

                Monro Capt RE
                OC 80th Fd Coy. RE
16.2.17

<u>After orders</u>:- The platoons of Fusiliers & Northants will move on the night 16-17 with all their kit to HESSIAN TR where they will be billetted until further orders. The Middlesex platoon will arrange to carry their tools & extra kit to their dug outs.

CRE 18th Div   APPENDIX F.
                                               Weekly progress report
From OC 80th Fd Coy. RE   Week ending Feb. 23. 1917

WORK	Date Commenced	MAP Location	PROGRESS
WIRING	17.2.17	abt R.11.c.44	100ˣ wire in front of Boom Ravine
	18.2.17	R.11.c.55	Strong point in front of Boom Ravine. Twining same. Completed
	20.2.17	R.11.c.64	Dug 30ˣ fire trench. Completed
Grid Walk	18.2.17		1 From junction of REGINA TR. and SUDBURY to BOOM RAVINE, last 200ˣ to be completed
			2 From HESSIAN Railhead to Boom RAVINE Via Valley. 170ˣ laid
			3 From ZOLLERN along SUDBURY to REGINA TR. ~~Grid about to~~ ~~along from Sudbury TR~~ about 400ˣ to complete.
Water Supply	21.2.17	NAB VALLEY	400ˣ of 4" piping uncovered on AUTHUILLE WOOD Water Supply.
Dugout	18.2.17	HESSIAN TR	Bunking. 13 beds erected. ~~completed~~
Strongpoint	17.2.17	R.11.c.24?	Strong point complete
Roads	21.2.17	GRANDCOURT Rd.	MILL Rd to BRIDGE Road. Road cleared of mud & water. Shell holes filled in & Surplus material moved ~~forward~~. About 50ˣ corduroying laid
Bunking		R24 Central	50 beds erected. ~~completed~~
Bath house	22.2.17	Crucifix Corner.	Cleaned out & levelled up floors.
Church Army Hut	22.2.17	WELLINGTON HUTS	Floor levelled.
Stores Hut	23.2.17	Coy HQ	Size 15' square. 80% completed.
Repairs	23.2.17	Colstand	Hut repairs. 30% complete
	23.2.17		

EHL JW.
for OC 80th Fd Coy RE
Lieut RE

A/6116 18th Division

APPENDIX G.
Weekly Progress Report

From / OC 80th Fd Coy RE   Week ending March 2. 17

WORK	Date Commenced	MAP Location	PROGRESS
Water Supply	21/2/17	NAB VALLEY	Completed. Water through to NAB Junction
Road	22/2/17	GRANDCOURT Rd	Building Grandcourt Rd from Mill Road to the North end of St Pierre Divion. 440ˣ run single width corduroy laid 100ˣ " double " " " 100ˣ " metal laid single width. 12 box culverts put in beneath road 300ˣ run drains cut. Excavation for single width complete 75% Completed for double width.
Wall Church	2/1/17	MARTINSART	Repairs to wall
Army Hut Repair	22/2/17	WELLINGTON Huts	80% Completed
	23/2/17	CABSTAND Huts	Completed
	24/2/17	Div Canteen	50% Completed
Baths	22/2/17	Crucifix Corner	Completed except for drains
Camp	2/1/17	W6 c0.4.	Camp 50% Completed.
Water Supply	2/1/17	Grandcourt Rd	Work Commenced.

2.3.17

M. Munnum.
Capt RE
OC 80th Fd Coy. RE

M/GRE 18th Division

APPENDIX G.
Weekly Progress Report

From / OC 80th Fd Coy RE   Week ending March 2. 17

WORK	Date Commenced	MAP Location	PROGRESS
Water Supply	21/2/17	NAB VALLEY	Completed. Hole through to NAB Junction
Road	22/2/17	Grandcourt Rd	Building Grandcourt Rd from Mill Road to the North end of St Pierre Divion.
			440 × run single width corduroy laid
			100 × " double " "
			100 × " metal laid single width
			12 box culverts put in beneath road
			300 × run drains cut.
			Excavation for single width complete
			75% completed for double width.
Wall	21/2/17	MARTINSART	Repairs to wall
Church Army Hut	22/2/17	WELLINGTON Huts	80% Completed
Repairs	23/2/17	CABSTAND Huts	Completed
	24/2/17	Div Canteen	50% completed
Baths	22/2/17	Crucifix Corner	Completed except for drain
Camp	2/3/17	W6 c.0.4.	Camp 50% Completed.
Water Supply	2/3/17	Grandcourt Rd	Work commenced.

2 · 3 · 17

OC 80th Fd Coy RE

Weekly progress report   APPENDIX. H.

80th Fd Coy RE   Week ending. 9.3.17

Work	date Commenced	Map Location	Progress.
Constructing Road	22/2/17	Grandcourt Rd from Mill road to N end of St Pierre Divion	Corduroy for single width and 50% double width complete. Side drains cut throughout entire length 3 box drains put in. Excavation complete.
Erecting Nissen Bow Huts	7/3/17	D. H.Q	5 Huts erected. complete
Making Road	8/3/17	- do -	40 yards run chalk laid. Site cleared
Building Stable	9/3/17	- do -	Work commenced.
Water Supply	2/3/17	Grandcourt Rd	Opened up water supply & erected 1 tank & pump. complete
Splitting Timber	2/3/17	- do -	Complete
Camp	2/3/17	Coy H.Q	80% completed
Baths	22/2/17	Crucifix Corner	Completed
	24/2/17	Div. Canteen	80% Completed
Chemical Army hut	22/3/17	Wellington Huts.	Completed
Fixing up	4/3/17	54 Bde H.Q	Completed.
Ammunition dump	5/3/17	Passerelle de Magenta.	80% Completed.
Platform	6/3/17	Refilling point	Completed

E Knight
Lieut RE
for OC 80 Fd Coy RE

Army Form C. 2118.

WAR DIARY or INTELLIGENCE SUMMARY

80 Bn Coy M.G.

(Erase heading not required.)

Nov 16

Place	Date	Hour	Summary of Events and Information	Remarks and references to Appendices
Coy H.Q. W.9.b.8.5.	1/3/17		For work see Appendix G. No 3 Section moved dugouts in Q.24.d.	G
Coy H.Q. M6.c.0.4	2/3/17		Coy H.Q.s + Hore lines + its attached platoon of MHarts moved to M6.c.0.4. No 2 Section + attached platoon of Mx. moved to Div Dump W.11.c.2.a. For work see Appendix G.	
	6/3/17		1st 4 Section + attached platoon of Beds moved to M.6.c.0.4. Attached platoon of MHarts moved to dugouts in Q.24.d.	
	7/3/17 To 9/3/17		See Appendix H.	M.H.
	10/3/17		2 Section Div Dump. 1 Section D.H.Q. stables etc. 1 Section Dugouts E. Miramont Rd. 2 M.G. Emplacements in front of Trys.	
	11/3/17		" 1 Section M.G. Emplacement in front of Trys.	
Coy H.Q. R.9.b.5.3.	12/3/17		Coy H.Q. + 2 Sections + platoon of MHarts moved to dugouts in GRANDCOURT. 2 Section + platoon of Mx, Beds + RF moved to dugouts in MIRAUMONT.	

WAR DIARY or INTELLIGENCE SUMMARY

Army Form C. 2118.

Place	Date	Hour	Summary of Events and Information	Remarks and references to Appendices
Coy H.Q. R.9.c.5.3	13/3/17		1 Section: Reconnoitring IRLES. 1 Section - Coy H.Q. 2 Section's Strong Pt. G.21.c.5.2, G.28.a.3.3	
	14/3/17		2 Sections Working Road thro' IRLES. 2 Sections Strong Pts. G.21.d.5.7. r.G.22.a.3.2.	
	15/3/17		1 Section Dugout Remaining IRLES. PYS, 1 Section sidewalk R.5.d.8.6. 1 " Strong Pt. G.21.d.5.7. 1 " strengthening cellars in MIRAUMONT.	
	16/3/17		2 Section Work on Dugout in IRLES. 1 Section work on Dugout in SOUTH MIRAUMONT TR. 1 " sidewalk R.5.d.8.6.	
Coy H.Q. R.5.a.8.1.	17/3/17		1 Section Sidewalk W of Pys. 3 Section standing by Coy. H.Q. & 2 Section & platoon of I/Hants move to MIRAUMONT.	
	18/3/17		1 Section making Fair Weather Track from G.26.c.3.7 to G.22.a.5.3. 3 Sections part of Advance Guard to B.54 Bde. move to BIHUCOURT.	
Coy. H.Q. G.17 Central	19/3/17		1 Section + attached Platoon making Fair Weather Track from L.35.d.4.6.to G.22.a.5.3. 1 Section reconnoitring wells in BIHUCOURT, ERVILLERS + ACHIET LE GRAND. 1 Section making tracks round crater in BIHUCOURT. 1 " " " " ERVILLERS.	
	20/3/17		ditto	
Coy H.Q. W.6.C.0.4.	21/3/17		Company moved back to W.6.C.0.4. Attached Platoons return to their Battalions	

Army Form C. 2118.

WAR DIARY
or
INTELLIGENCE SUMMARY

(Erase heading not required.)

Instructions regarding War Diaries and Intelligence Summaries are contained in F. S. Regs., Part II. and the Staff Manual respectively. Title Pages will be prepared in manuscript.

Place	Date	Hour	Summary of Events and Information	Remarks and references to Appendices
Coy HQ. VADENCOURT.	22/3/17		Company marched to VADENCOURT.	
MONTONVILLERS	23/3/17		Company march to MONTONVILLERS.	
DURY.	24/3/17		Dismounted section of the Company bus to DURY. Transport ~ march ~	
"	25/3/17		Rest.	
SALEUX Railway Station	26/3/17		Company march to SALEUX.	
"	27/3/17		Company entrain for STEENBECQUE.	
GAUBECQUE.	28/3/17		Company detrain at STEENBECQUE & march to billets at GAUBECQUE.	
	29/3/17		TRAINING.	
	30/3/17		Ditto.	
	31/3/17		Ditto.	

J.Murphy Lt R.E.
for O.C. 80th Field Coy R.E.

WAR DIARY or INTELLIGENCE SUMMARY

Army Form C. 2118

18 Div — GOFERE — Vol II

XXII

Place	Date	Hour	Summary of Events and Information	Remarks and references to Appendices
BRAY.	April 1st		80 Field Co. R.E. Company H.Q. and N° 1 Section working in BRAY at 21° Boulevarders, Workshops etc. Bay at in BRAY. N° 2 Section working in A.2 Sector. N° 4 " " " " The men in Bryant in CATTET WOOD BRICK ALLEY. 2 Officers living in Bryant just off BRICK ALLEY. N° 3 Section at work on Army Post (nearing completion) and Water Supply and New Communications CANNOT SHEFFIELD and PERONNE AVENUE, also BILLON WOOD WELLS man balustrade. All details of works are contained in Summary at End of Diary.	
	2nd 3rd	1630	Nothing unusual to report "	
	29th		Health of Company in General has been Excellent. 1 Mounted L Cpl. wounded with crock shew working Gunnas on the 29th met with Reception No. 2 Section marched to QUERRIEN under XIII Corps for duty The Company went under Canvas in the trenches.	
	28th		N° 2 Section relieved by N° 1 Section in A.2 Sector	

WAR DIARY
or
INTELLIGENCE SUMMARY

Army Form C. 2118

Place	Date	Hour	Summary of Events and Information	Remarks and references to Appendices
	April 30		80th Field Coy RE.	
			No 2 Section relieved by No 3 Section in A.1. Sector.	
			Summary of work done by Company during month of April.	
			Front line Dugouts and Shelters.	
			A.1. Sector	
			19 Parapet Shelters for Sentry posts ⎫	
			7 Corrugated Iron Shelters 8ft × 6ft ⎬ in or just behind front line	
			2 Steel Shelting have been completed ⎭	
			5 Corrugated Iron Shelters 8ft × 6ft ⎫ ditto	
			2 Steel Shelters are in hand ⎭	
			A.2. Sector	
			25 Parapet Shelters for Sentry posts ⎫	
			10 Corrugated Iron Shelters 8ft × 6ft ⎬ ditto	
			5 Steel Shelters have been completed ⎭	
			3 Corrugated Iron Shelters 8ft × 6ft ⎫ ditto	
			1 Steel Shelter in hand ⎭	

80th Field Coy?

WAR DIARY
or
INTELLIGENCE SUMMARY.

April 1917 Folio 1

Place	Date	Hour	Summary of Events and Information	Remarks and references to Appendices
GUARBECQUE (PAS de CALAIS)	1-4-17		Training	
	2-4-17		Divisional General - Major General Lee inspected the Company at training	
	3/4/17		do	
	do		Training	
	8/4/17			
	9.4.17		Took part in Divisional Horse show. Training	
	10.4.17 to 15.4.17		Training	
	16.4.17		C.E. II Corps inspected the Company. Company moved to billets in THIENNES to take part in Brigade exercise on 17th	
	17.4.17		Brigade exercise cancelled. Company returned to billets in GUARBECQUE. Training	
	18.4.17			
	19.4.17		Company prepared to move to billets in THIENNES for Brigade exercise but Brigade exercise cancelled.	
	20.4.17		Training	

Army Form C. 2118.

WAR DIARY
or
INTELLIGENCE SUMMARY.

(Erase heading not required.)

April 1917. Folio 2.

Place	Date	Hour	Summary of Events and Information	Remarks and references to Appendices
BUSNES (Pas du Calais)	21.4.17		Company moved to billets in BUSNES	
	22.4.17 to 25.4.17		Training	
PRESSY LES PERNES	26.4.17		Company moved with 54th Div. late to billets in PRESSY-LES-PERNES	
	27.4.17		Dismounted portion of the Company moved to NEUVILLE VITASSE by train and road	
			Transport marched to BEAURAINS by road	
NEUVILLE VITASSE and BEAURAINS	28.4.17		Dismounted portion of Company moved to point N26 c.o.5. on the NEUVILLE VITASSE — HENIN Road	
N26.c.o.5.	29.4.17		Transport and Mounted Section joined the Company at point N26 c.o.5.	
			3 Section worked on road from NEUVILLE to St MARTIN.	
			1 Section worked on camp	
			4 Section worked on Road.	
	30.4.17		Dismounted portion of Company moved to point N.28.d.3.3. (near MÉNINEL)	

Maurice W. ayr RE

WAR DIARY
or
INTELLIGENCE SUMMARY.
(Erase heading not required.)

Army Form C. 2118.

80 Fd Coy R.E.
May 1917

Place	Date	Hour	Summary of Events and Information	Remarks and references to Appendices
	1/5/17	–	Transport in NEUVILLE VITASSE at Point N.26.C.05.	Folio. No. 1. May 1918
NEUVILLE VITASSE	1/5/17	–	Dismounted portion of Company in bivouacs in a trench (N.28.a.3.3.)	
	2/5/17		No 1 & 4 section work in Batt. Hd. Qr. dugouts	
	2/5/17		No 2 Sec work on walks point – HENINEL and helping in 3 brick wire roads	
	3/5/17		and forward dumps	
			bivouac Camp	
	4/5/17		Making dry weather tracks from N.29 central to N.31.a central	
	5/5/17		No 1 Section making dry weather tracks from N.36.a central to N.31.a central. No 2 T.H.	
	6/5/17		section work on dugouts N.30.b. No 3 See improving Camp	
	7/5/17		ditto	
	7/5/17		No 3 Sec making dry weather tracks from N.29 central to M.36.a central. No 1 T.H. sec. on 5" 6"	

WAR DIARY or INTELLIGENCE SUMMARY

Army Form C. 2118

Place	Date	Hour	Summary of Events and Information	Remarks and references to Appendices
H.Q. L.g.c.a.v.	BRAY		80th Field Coy R.E.	
	1st - 31st		The Company has been under Canvas during the month; with exception of the Sections in trenches. One Section at a time has been sent back to CHIPILLY to the Divisional R.E. rest camp; and remain 10 days there. The Sections have been inoculated, and have been put through training during the morning, consisting of Musketry, Bombing, Bayonet fighting, Rapid wiring, and Pontooning, etc. Well made appreciated by the men. The health of the Company has been fair, but sickness has been above normal.	
			Casualties — 2 killed	
			2 wounded sick.	
			13 admitted Hospital.	
			8 discharged.	

WAR DIARY
or
INTELLIGENCE SUMMARY

Army Form C. 2118

(Erase heading not required.)   folio 2.

Place	Date	Hour	Summary of Events and Information	Remarks and references to Appendices

May.

The Company has had during the month

1 Section on Extension and alteration to SUZANNE - CARNOY water
Supply.
Protection to Pumping Station by Sandbag walls at SUZANNE.
Alterations to Main Storage Reservoir at CONTOUR WOOD.
Re erection of 2 - 3200 gallon tanks and protection of same and relaying 840 yards of 2" galvanised piping taken over from 1/3rd Durham RE.

2 Sections Trench work in A. and B. Sub Sectors

BRONFAY
Increasing Dugout accommodation in CARNOY and BRONFAY FARM.
Work on hand in general repair and strengthening
1 Dugout for 50 Infantry   30
19   "   "   "   "   560
1   "   "   "   "   30
1   "   "   "   Officers
2   "   "   "   Cookhouses
1   "   "   "   Artillery Exchange

CARNOY
Dugouts for two Battns. 500 men in tunnel.

Army Form C. 2118

WAR DIARY
or
INTELLIGENCE SUMMARY
(Erase heading not required.)

Folio 2

Instructions regarding War Diaries and Intelligence Summaries are contained in F. S. Regs., Part II. and the Staff Manual respectively. Title Pages will be prepared in manuscript.

Place	Date	Hour	Summary of Events and Information	Remarks and references to Appendices
	May		Communication Trenches.	
			PIONEER AVENUE . . 1000 yards widened.	
			MAIDSTONE AVENUE . 55	
			Front Line.	
			100 yards revetted trenches dug by 3 Section at A/7/4	

B Chamberlain
Capt
for O.C. 2nd Coy R.E.

80 2nd Coy R.E. Army Form C. 2118
XVIII Vol 7
June folio 1.

WAR DIARY
or
INTELLIGENCE SUMMARY
(Erase heading not required.)

Instructions regarding War Diaries and Intelligence Summaries are contained in F.S. Regs., Part II. and the Staff Manual respectively. Title Pages will be prepared in manuscript.

Place	Date	Hour	Summary of Events and Information	Remarks and references to Appendices
BRAY			80th Field Company, R.E.	
H.Q. L.9.c.4.2	June 1st	—	With the exception of men in Trenches the Company remains under canvas.	
			No 1 & 2 Sections are living in Trenches in front of CARNOY.	
			No 3 Section and by subs at BRONFAY FARM engaged in water supply.	
			No 4 Section being in Rest-Camp at CHIPILLY undergoing training.	
	8th		No 1 Section changing with No 4 Section at Rest-Camp	
	15th		No 1 Section returned to trenches owing to urgency of work before No 2 Section. The Company, less 15 men to work in Divisional Workshops on Trench bridges, Maltings, and assisting RE Stores in mass loads for forward RE Dumps in trenches in front of CARNOY	
	23rd		No 1 and 4 Section returned to Company H.Q. for rest.	
	28th		No 1 Section returned to Company H.Q.	
			No 2 and 4 Sections on standing by for zero day	
			No 3 Section continue on maintenance of Suzanne Canvoy water supply.	
"	30th		No 2 and 4 Sections up to trenches, leaving Camp at 6.30 pm to stand by for zero.	

WAR DIARY or INTELLIGENCE SUMMARY

Army Form C. 2118

Place	Date	Hour	Summary of Events and Information	Remarks and references to Appendices
June	1		Following work has been carried out by 90th Field Coy. R.E. this month.	folio v.
			<u>Accommodation</u> at Bronfay Farm Repair to 30 Dugouts.	
			<u>Water Supply</u>	
			31st	
			3 30m (allen?) Tanks was completed at Contour Wood and political with Sandbag Walls and Timber Log roofing. service of bursting Sandbags finished.	
			4 1600 galln Steel Tanks erected in CARNOY 2 at A.14.a.1.5. 2 at A.13.d.w.9.	
			Laying 650 yards of 2" Main from F.18.a.9.3. to 57th Bde. Dump at F.18.a.9.3.	
			Maintenance of SUZANNE - CARNOY Water Supply.	
	Bryoli		Right and Left Battalion Advanced H.Q. for 54th Bde. at 3rd Battalion Advanced H.Q. at PICCADILLY at 7.m.c. 9.12/2 and A.7/14	
			Also 3 Tunnelled dugouts include accommodation for Signals.	
			2 Dugouts on Road PT 104 - CARNOY.	
			1 6" Stokes Mortar Amm Store. in CARNOY on MONTAUBAN Rd.	

WAR DIARY
or
INTELLIGENCE SUMMARY

Army Form C. 2118

Place	Date	Hour	Summary of Events and Information	Remarks and references to Appendices
	1		Arrangements and fitting, and supervision of filling	
			2 Advanced Dumps for RE Material	
			Bombs } from line so Pole Trank	
			S.A.A. }	
			Tools } in PICCADILLY	
			Site	
			1 in GEORGE STREET at JUNCTION with PIONEER AVENUE	
			1 Surface Dump PIONEER AVENUE	
			Communications	
			Completion of 1700* deepening, gridding	
			Approximately { 800* } of trench deepened for full cover. Their	
			{ 3000* } gridded and drained	
			work on chiefly in a forming up lines and with communications	
			Cherry and Bridge Sites	
			Tu MANETZ - CARNOY road. 5 bridges	
			Road from A.3.b.0.3 to F.12.a.9.3	
			Pont roux - CARNOY Road bridged A.12.b.6.3. a bridge	
			Cutting out steps & all forming of trenches	
			and affixing Latrines for same	

WAR DIARY
or
INTELLIGENCE SUMMARY

Army Form C. 2118

(Erase heading not required.)

Place	Date	Hour	Summary of Events and Information	Remarks and references to Appendices
June	1		300 Burials for Traffic on BRAY - CARNOY RD in CARNOY Cemetery completed. Making and painting all Notice Boards for Enemy Trench on 524.5 Objective and our own communications and forming up lines etc. have been completed in all. 600 Notice boards Repaired heads and Spirit of Company report. Casualties. Evacuated Sick 3. O.R. Admitted to Hospital 4. O.R. and 1 Officer. Discharged from Field Clearing Station 7. O.R. Wounded 3. O.R. Shell Shock 2. O.R. Killed 1. O.R.	

B. Chamberlayne
Capt. R.E.

WAR DIARY or INTELLIGENCE SUMMARY

Army Form C. 2118

folio 3

80th Field Coy R.E.

Two Company H.Q. Dug out completed in A. Sector in COKE and CUMBERLAND AVENUES

100' of Railway line removed at A 9/4 completed.

New Communication Digging.

FUSILIER TRENCH	450' Berm cleared	50' widened
MERCASTON AVENUE	600'	5' – 700' 5' – 800' deepened
SUNKEN ROAD	Aug 3' × 3' – 430'	
FUSILIER AVENUE	" 5' – 600'	
	" – 560'	
CARNOY AVENUE		
NEW TRENCH from	" 3' × 3' – 240'	
BURHAM TRENCH to BATTLE H.Q.s	" – 120'	
		250' S

Grids in French floors.

MAIDSTONE AVENUE	250' laid
FRANCIS AVENUE	150'
TRENCH 1. (LONDON RD FRANCE STEET TO PORTLAND AV)	55'
TRENCH 2. (FRANCIS AV - MAIDSTONE AV)	480"
CARNOY AVENUE	450' laid
SHEFFIELD AVENUE	250'

WAR DIARY
or
INTELLIGENCE SUMMARY

(Erase heading not required.)

Army Form C. 2118

80th Field Co. RE.

No 3 Army Survey post completed.

5 Dugouts in BRONFAY FARM DETATCHT under repair; and cellars strengthened

4 CHARTON HORST have been erected for 54th Div. for Gas alarms

BATHS erected at BRONFAY FARM.

14th Sep/16.
1300 x 5" main removed to be replaced by 4"
650 x 2" main laid } for branches to supply Brigade and Batteries
800 x 1" "   }   along line of tram. (4")

Erection of Ablution benches and stand pipes Bicam wood
Construction Ferro concrete Tanks in CARNOY
various 100 and 200 gallon Tanks erected along lines of main to improve distribution to various units.

100' TRAMWAY laid from BRAY-FRICOURT Railway to 83rd RE Southwards.

Army Form C. 2118

WAR DIARY
or
INTELLIGENCE SUMMARY
(Erase heading not required.)

folio 5.

Place	Date	Hour	Summary of Events and Information	Remarks and references to Appendices

80th Field Coy RE.

Coy RE. Workshops and Sandbags.

25 Rat Pea. Pump made.
3   Rifle Grenade Battery Stands
80 Parapet shelters
210 Trench gratings (with waste material)
250 Notice Boards of various kinds
18 Window frames
3   Range observation periscopes
4   Office Tables
2   Printing frames for maps
5   Carpenters benches.

The Company has handed over } Waterloo
during the 29th and 30th   } Farm,
                                } Stable,
                                } Billets,
                                } Cookhouse
                                } and Officer
                                 1/5 The 202nd RE. 30th Div.

B. Chambers
Capt. RE.

WAR DIARY
or
INTELLIGENCE SUMMARY

(Erase heading not required.)

Army Form C. 2118.

86" Fd Cy R.E.

June 1917

Folio 1

Place	Date	Hour	Summary of Events and Information	Remarks and references to appendices
Cy HQ & 4 Section M26.	1/6/17 to 2/6/17		15ec. Dugouts M136.d.8.6. 15ec. Dugouts O.31.C.2.7. 15ec Mining Shaft. TR. 15ec. Intermediate Line. Forming Army M36.6.6.A. A.D.S. M.28.c.4.3. Diggs Bush TR. Winning Pulp Lane.	
Havelines M25.d.9.5.	3/6/17 7/6/17		Ditto	Ditto
	8/6/17		Ditto	Ditto
	9/6/17		Ditto + Inf Bde HQ at M35.C.3.3.	Ditto + Diggs Shaft at V.1.C.0.3. Ditto
	11/6/17		15ec Dugouts M36.d.8.6. 15ec Inf Bde HQ at M35.C.3.3. 15ec Sap V.1.C.0.3. Sap U.1.a.	Ditto
	12/6/17 to 16/6/17		Ditto	Ditto + O.P. & Shaft Tr. Ditto
Gaudiempré	17/6/17 18/6/17 to 20/6/17		Company marched to GAUDIEMPRÉ. Training	
Devonshire Camp Ouderdom	21/6/17 22/6/17		Company entrained at SAULTY & detrained at POPERINGHE marched to DEVONSHIRE CAMP OUDERDOM.	

Army Form C. 2118.

WAR DIARY
or
INTELLIGENCE SUMMARY
(Erase heading not required.)

80th Fd Coy RE

June 1917   Folio 2

Place	Date	Hour	Summary of Events and Information	Remarks and references to Appendices
Sheet 28 NW. H26.6.8.2. J.23.	6/17		Secs N° 2-4. marched & camped at H.30.6. central.	
	24/6/17		H.Qrs. Sec N°3 - transport marched & camped at H.26.6. central.	
			Officers & Sergeants reconnoitre forward trenches running from WOODCOTE	
			House I.20.c.5.2. to ZILLEBEKE I.22.6.8.0	
	25/6/17		Officers & Sergeants reconnoitre communication trench at I.15.d.2.3. which	
			was in bad state of repair. N°3 Section Training.	
	27/6/17 to 28/6/17		Commenced Work on trench at I.15.d.2.3. N°3 Section Training	
	29/6/17 30/6/17		Ditto. N°3 Section relieve N°2 Section Training	

Major H Warren RE
for Major RE
O.C. 80th Fd Coy RE

Army Form C. 2118.

WAR DIARY
or
INTELLIGENCE SUMMARY.

(Erase heading not required.)

May 1917   Folio 3

Place	Date	Hour	Summary of Events and Information	Remarks and references to Appendices
	28/6/17		No 1 Sec Constructing dugouts at junction BROWN & AVENUE Trenches U.36.d.86. No 2 Sec "worth a dugout" trenches O.31.C.2.7. and Shelters at Corner cut crossing Station N.28.d.4.3.	
	6		No 3 Sec Digging dipt from SHAFT Trench U.1.C.0.8. and digging No SM Trench flats See "Mining Intermediate" Line and building grounds to St Louis field office.	
	3/5/17			

M. Munro
Major R.E.
O.C. 80th Fd Coy R.E.

Headquarters,
  18th Division.
================

           Herewith War Diary of the
80th Field Company, R.E, for the month of
July, 1916.

                              B Chambers
                                  Captain.
5/8/16.
        Adjutant, 18th Divisional Engineers.

Army Form C. 2118.

Vol 2 o
80 Fd Coy RE

WAR DIARY
or
INTELLIGENCE SUMMARY.
(Erase heading not required.)

Place	Date	Hour	Summary of Events and Information	Remarks and references to Appendices
Sheet 28 NW.	July 1917		Folio 1.	
	1/7		Coy. Hd Qrs & Horse lines T.10.2 Lat at H.26.6. central	
			No 1, 3 & 4 Sec at H.29.d. central	
	2/7		No 2 Section training. 1 & 3 Section work on C.T. N side of ZILLEBEKE Lake	
	3/7		ditto. ditto. moved Camp to H.23.a.	
	4/7		1 & 2 Section work on Ad 30 D. H.Q. 3 & 4 Section ditto	
	5/7		1 Sec moved back to Coy H.Q. 2, 3 & 4. ditto	
	6/7		3 & 4 Section moved back to Coy H.Q. 1 or 2	
	7/7		2 Section on Ad 30 & 1.15" D.H.Q. and work on Div Dump H.33.6. Dickebusch	
	8/7		Making mule mats and attachments for Gr. Saddles for pack animals to new loads	
	10/7		2 Section improving accomodation & dugouts T.20.65.a. Revetting T10 emplacents	
			Observatory Ridge and work on C.T. N side of ZILLEBEKE LAKE. All 6 Sec Trot	
	16/7		2 Sec at H.Q. relieved 2 Section its forward areas where TM emplacements	
	23/7		completed. Work commenced on Road post. C.T. etc.	
	24/7		Sections returned to Coy H.Q. work on Ad D.H.Q. & Div Dump	

WAR DIARY
or
INTELLIGENCE SUMMARY.

(Erase heading not required.)

Army Form C. 2118.

May 1917   Folio 2

Place	Date	Hour	Summary of Events and Information	Remarks and references to Appendices
	8/5/17		No 1 Sec work on dugouts for Survey Coy at N27a. No 3 Sec work on intermediate line	
	9/5/17		No 2 & 4 Sec work on dugouts N30b as at 5', 6' & 7'	
	10/5/17		ditto	
	11/5/17		Nos 1 & 3 Sec ditto. No 2 & 4 work on intermediate line	
	12/5/17		No 1, 2 & 3 Sec ditto. No 4 Sec work on Brown Trench	
	13/5/17		as 11/5/17 also work on dug out trolley line at N35e	
	14/5/17		ditto also work on Advanced Dressing Station N28c Sohell?	
	15/5/17		ditto also work on R.E. dump (MENIN)	
	16/5/17			
	17/5/17		No 1 Sec on dugouts Brown Trench No 2 Sec on intermediate line, also dug outs	
	18/5/17		Trench N35S.E. and Advanced Dressing Station N28C, also 3 Sec on intermediate line	
	19/5/17		No 4 Sec on Brown Trench. Also work on Saving Tornado dumps N36 c.64.	
	20/5/17		ditto also Bridging trench N29d for dug outs, Faith and digging Telechy	
	21/5/17		Bush Trench T Sap VI c. and Hippodrome Support T6 c 26 T 27	

Army Form C. 2118.

WAR DIARY
or
INTELLIGENCE SUMMARY.
(Erase heading not required.)

20th Field Coy R.E.

Aug 1917 Folio 1 Vol 21

Place	Date	Hour	Summary of Events and Information	Remarks and references to Appendices
Mears PN Coy HQ H.33.c	1/7		Coy disbd of Hd Coy	
	2/7 6 a/m			
	3/7		2 Section with R.2 attacked Station of infantry moved to INCIDENT DUMP	
	4/7		2 Section arrived at Coy Hd Conference in Camp	
	7/9/7		2 Section attacked infantry preparing dumps and roads for operations and return to Coy H.Q. 10.8.17. 2 Section left Coy HQ for assembly positions where they remained until 4 am 11.8.17. No work was done and they returned to the Plater Dugout Area No 4	
	12/7		2 Section left Plater Square area to maintain Junc 49 & J.14 a 5.6 and returned in to Coy Hd Coys on the morning 13/7	
	13/7		2 Section left Coy Hd Coys for the line in order to finish the circuit # not quite completed the night before and returning to Coy HQ early morning of 14/7	
	15/7		Dismounted Patrol of Coy preceded by lorry to LE PARADIS arr 27. Mounted proceeded by road and arrived at destination 16/7/17	
	16/7	6.30	Coy billetted at LE PARADIS for rest & training	

Army Form C. 2118.

WAR DIARY
or
INTELLIGENCE SUMMARY.

(Erase heading not required.)

80th Fd Coy RE

Summary of Events and Information Folio 2. July 1917

Place	Date	Hour	Summary of Events and Information	Remarks and references to Appendices
	28/7		3 Sections working on Adv D.H.Q. improvements to camps, duckboards etc.	
	to		1 Section on forward dumps	
	29/7		—	
	30/7		Coy rested	
	31/7		Operation. Coy moved to Cholera Sugar area but owing to failure of tabs, part of operation they were not required and returned to Coy Hd Qrs in the evening.	

H. Blandy Major
OC 80 Fd Coy RE

WAR DIARY
INTELLIGENCE SUMMARY

Army Form C. 2118.

Place	Date	Hour	Summary of Events and Information	Remarks and references to Appendices
RONSSOY	29/9	8am	No. 1. 2. 3. Sections assembled in RIDGE RESERVE TR. In readiness	
		6pm	Took over BRIDGES VENDHUILLE E.3.a 2.6 8ll G2c GUYENCOURT.	
	30/9	10am	Commenced reconnaissance of St. QUENTIN CANAL in Wings VENDHUILLE	
	30/9	12 midday	Company assembled at RIDGE RESERVE TR. F.15.b & 3 (G2c)	
	30/9	9pm	Reconnaissance of CANAL CROSSINGS Company returned to GUYENCOURT. Casualties 3 O.R wounded.	

Ospar Naipak
O. C. No. C Coy R.E.

Army Form C. 2118.

WAR DIARY
or
INTELLIGENCE SUMMARY.
(Erase heading not required.)

80 H/Q Coy 116 September 1917 Folio Vol 22

Place	Date	Hour	Summary of Events and Information	Remarks and references to Appendices
PETIT PARAIS	1/9/17		Rest & Training	
LE PARAIS	2/9/17			
	3/17		Coy moved to Billets at C.26.d.1.6. near LEDRINGHEM Sheet 27 1/40,000	
Ledringhem	4/17		Rest & Training	
	15/17			
	13/17		2 Sections moved to BONNINGUES for work under XIX Corps	
			2 " " "	
	14/17		2 Sections working under XIX Corps at BONNINGUES.	
	16-22/17		2 Sections Training	
	23/17		No.1 Section working on Batts at C.17.c.3.8. near WORMHOUDT Sheet 27 1/40,000	
			No.2 Section working under XIX Corps at BONNINGUES.	
			2 Sections working under XIX Corps at BONNINGUES.	
	24/17		2 Sections working under XIX Corps at BONNINGUES.	
			2 Sections Training	
	25/17		2 Sections working under XIX Corps at BONNINGUES.	
			2 Sections working on Batts at C.17.c.3.8. near WORMHOUDT Sheet 27 1/40,000	

WAR DIARY or INTELLIGENCE SUMMARY

Army Form C. 2118.

80th Fd. Coy. R.E.

September 1917 Folio 1.

Place	Date	Hour	Summary of Events and Information	Remarks and references to Appendices
LEDRINGHEM	26/9		2 Sections working under XIX Corps at BONNINGUES.	
	to 27/9		2 Sections Training	
	28/9		Nos 1 and 2 Secs. proceeded by Busses to Camp at B.22.d.8.1. Sheet 27. 1/40000	
Coy. H.Q. B.22.d.8.1.			Nos. 3 and 4 Secs proceeded by lorries from BONNINGUES, and joined Coy. at B.22.d.8.1.	
			Mounted Section of Coy. proceeded by road to A.21.a.8.7. Sheet 27. 1/40000	
	29/9		1 Section working on Camp B.22.d.8.1.	
			3 Sections working on Stables B.22.d.8.1.	
	30/9		2 Sections working on Camp B.22.d.8.1.	
			2 Sections working on Stables B.22.d.8.1.	

[signature]
Captain R.E.
for O.C. 80th Field Coy. R.E.

WAR DIARY or INTELLIGENCE SUMMARY

Army Form C. 2118.

Vol 23

80th Ft Coy R.E.   Oct/Nov 1917

Place	Date	Hour	Summary of Events and Information	Remarks and references to Appendices
Sheet 28 NW Coy Ht Qrs B.32.c.8.1. Transport at A.21.a.8.7.	1/11/17		1 Section worked on Camp improvements TC and 3 Section worked on erecting staffs in vicinity of camp.	
	6/11/17 9/11/17	9.10		
	10/11/17	10.10	Dismounted portion of Coy moved to Camp near Coy Hd Qrs at C.25.a.7.6. with forward location at B.32.d.3.6.	
	11/11/17		1 Section work on billet &c. 3 Section work on "S" duck board track. Maintenance improvement Tellussin.	
	12/11/17		Dismounted portion of Coy work on "S" duck board track.	
	6/15/17			
	16/17		3 Section on "S" track. 1 Section on CAMP shelter U.30.d.	2 OR Wounded 16/11/17
	17/17		1 Section on "S" track. 1 Section on CAMP shelter. 2 Section work on POELCAPELLE Rd. C6.	1 OR Wounded 17/11/17 C.6.
	18/17		Coy worked on "S" grid track. CAMP shelter and work on dugouts & drainage C.9.a.	2 OR Wounded C.9.a.
			in CAMP Post and Tramway also POELCAPELLE Rd. C6.	
	19/17		In addition to above work on VARNA Fm (Bde HQ) and forming forward dump of RE material in U.30.d. also CAMP shelter at V.25.a. work on shelter at U.30.d Complete.	2 OR Wounded 19/10/17

Army Form C. 2118.

WAR DIARY
or
INTELLIGENCE SUMMARY.

(Erase heading not required.)

80th Fld Coy R.E.   Folio 2.

Place	Date	Hour	Summary of Events and Information	Remarks and references to Appendices
	20/10/17	5"	"B" Grid hard laid forward. Work on maintenance & improvement. Testuvier	
	21/10/17		do as a.19	
	22/10/17		"B" Grid hard laid forward. Work on maintenance & improvement. Testuvier forming forward dumps at MINTY FM, erecting R.A.M.C. Shelter C25a, Improvements to VARNA FM, drainage &c of CANE POST and repairs to	
	23/10/17		CANAL BANK. C25a.	
	24/10/17		Dismounted portion of Company moved to B.19.d.4.2 - received Hospital FM. Forward Sections relieved to transport Lines at A21.a.6.7. 1 Officer & 3 OR Wounded	25.10.17
	25/10/17		Dismounted portion of Company moved to CANAL BANK C13.a.19	
	26/10/17		Transport moved to A.11.b.44. took over Lorries from 77th Fd Coy R.E.	
	27/10/17		Dismounted portion of Coy took over work from 77th Fd Coy R.E. and worked on erection of Nissen Bow Huts at ROSE and HUDDLESTONE Camps. C.I.a. and C7d. 2 OR Killed 6 OR	
			Wounded 29/10/17. 1 OR Wounded 29/10/17.	
	28 & 31/10/17		Work as a 24.10.17.	
			Wounded 30/10/17	

M. Munro
Major R.E.
O.C. 80th Fd Coy R.E.

WAR DIARY
INTELLIGENCE SUMMARY
(Erase heading not required.) Sheet

Army Form C. 2118.

S.O. 7th Cav. B.S.

November 1917.

Vol 24

Place	Date	Hour	Summary of Events and Information	Remarks and references to Appendices
Sheet 28.N.W. Coy HQ. 7 Dismounts at C.13.a.19. Canal Post Transport at B.13.6.8.4.	1-4/17		Work on erecting Nissen Huts in Lieu of Subalterns Camp at C.13.C.7d.	
	5/17		Company moved Dismounts HQ & Camp B.9.a Horselines at B.13.6.8.4	
	6/17		Work on Huts & Nissens at Dismount Camp B.9. Improvement of Horse Camp and protection for Lines at Transport Lines.	
	7/17 & 8/17		As above also work commenced by 2 Sections making new Camp at Camel Bank B.6.C.82.	
	9/17		Section in Dismount Camp occupied to 2 Sections at new Camp B.6.C.82 erecting Nissens	
	6		Pitchers near Camp. Remainder of Company erecting Nissen Huts at N.A.O.R.S. Camp B.9.C.	
	11/17		and clearing the Broomager & the Steenbeek Fallen the water to obtain supply.	
	12/17		as 9/k/11" also bridging across the Steenbeek at Railways - Charge St	
	13/17		as above. Bridge over Steenbeek complete. 3 Section moved to new Camp at Canal Bank N6.C.82.	
	14/17 & 15/17		Work as for 7/11 Nissen Camp Complete 15/11/17. In addition work was undertaken on Causeway across Steenbeek, drying Sheets in the Broomager Valley and repair to Duckwalks.	

Army Form C. 2118.

WAR DIARY
or
INTELLIGENCE SUMMARY.
(Erase heading not required.)

Sheet 2. November 1917

Instructions regarding War Diaries and Intelligence Summaries are contained in F. S. Regs., Part II. and the Staff Manual respectively. Title pages will be prepared in manuscript.

Place	Date	Hour	Summary of Events and Information	Remarks and references to Appendices
	19/11		Coy. 7 new survey shewards moved to new Camp Canal Bank.	
	20/11		Work at Canterbury T. during above Coy held up. Coy took over work in the line from 79th Fd Coy R.E.	
	T		Work. 2 Sections on ROEUINCRE RD dump making maintenance of the material and supervisory transport of same to RRE dump at Roeux Rd – HUNTER St. U.17.a.0.2 also work on camp improvements &c	
	21/11		2 Section on Highland Constructing duckwalks in the forest posts $\{14$ and $16\}$ completed 21/11 U.5.b.	
	22/11		No work forward owing to relief other work as 20/11.	
	23/11	Night	1 Section supervising the wiring of the main line of defence Toulzac lines a left.	
			" Erecting M.G. Cy shelter. 1 supervising work & outpost line & right.	
	T		1 " in extension of Camp. 1 Section taking taking baby elephants & Area U.17.a.	
	24/11		also detailed sappers to carry wiring & dumping materials up from 20"/17	
	25/11		Work on machine gun on ROEUINCRE dump and guiding carrying parties with stores to FAID HERBE CROSS ROADS U.5.d.8... Lilly gas screen. Battalion Fighter line. also work on MACHINE gun wiring continued.	

WAR DIARY
INTELLIGENCE SUMMARY
(Erase heading not required.)

Army Form C. 2118.

About 3 November 1917

Place	Date	Hour	Summary of Events and Information	Remarks and references to Appendices
	26/11/17		Work as on 25/11/17 also extension H.Q. Camp & continuation of making & dumping new loads of R.E. material.	
	27/11/17 28/11/17		Casualties — 2 O.R.s wounded 26/11/17. Work on Camp construction & new loads at dump as usual. Also camouflage screens. No work forward owing to relief.	
	29/11/17		Work as on 28/11/17 Coy. still making & dumping forward camouflage screens, extensive Camp making & dumping new loads of R.E. material and supervising wiring in the line carried on with as on 28th.	
	30/11/17		After detailed work on improving dopping and making new loads at dumps. Remainder of Coy. — 4 Section & B attached platoon of Infantry employed at night 1200 yds of camouflage near the road from U.5.c.23.6. U.6.d.07.	

[signature] Maj RE
O.C. 8th Coy RE

WAR DIARY
INTELLIGENCE SUMMARY

Army Form C. 2118.

80 Z⁰ Coy R.E.
December 1917 Vol 925

Place	Date	Hour	Summary of Events and Information	Remarks and references to Appendices
b/36.c.8.2.	1/12	—	Work on dumps at SOESINGHE, making new loads T.C. T getting same to forward dumps	
Nieupot	2/12		ditto also deepening T.covering mass defensive line and	
Nieupot	3/12		extending the Coy camp i.e making Subs T	
No 6 & 4	4/12		ditto also erecting shelter at Sable house O.SL 9.3 and	
	5/12		Sec Lieut O.11.6.8.6 (that 20.) Mullin explied	
	6		Wiring main defence line. Work in dump NOESINGHE T getting materials	
	15/12		Thematerial forward to KOEKUIT Ad dump. Extension of Camp. Wiring string	
	15/12		be nts CA St	
	16/12		Coy moved to MACINGHE Area (octive X 13 a 30 sheet 19.	
	6		Rest T Training. One Section moved to Fix Corps Reinforcement Camps	
	31/12		O.18.c.9 for dumps erecting Subs VI. T returned to Coy a 28.c.2	

Signed Capt R.E.
for O.C. 80 Z⁰ Coy R.E.

WAR DIARY or INTELLIGENCE SUMMARY.

Army Form C. 2118.

80th Field Coy R.E.

Vol 26

Place	Date	Hour	Summary of Events and Information	Remarks and references to Appendices
X.13.a.3.0 Sheet 19	1/1/18	—	Company moved to BOESINGHE AREA LOCATION B.6.c.8.2. Sheet 28. Transport to B.13.b.6.4. Sheet 28. Commenced w/c on inward communications, repairs to roads, light Railway and Duckboard tracks.	
	3/1/18	—	3 Casualties. 2 O.R. sick. 1. O.R. wounded.	
	4/1/18	—	Maintenance of Roads.	
	11/1/18	—	Commenced w/c on MARTINS MILL – TUFFS BRIDGE ROAD.	
	10/1/18	—	Erection of Camouflage Screen CORPS DEFENSIVE LINE U.17a. Sheet 20 U.20.d. Sheet 20.	
	12/1/18	—	Erected Accommodation for 1 Company in CORPS DEFENSIVE LINE U.11.c. Sheet 20.	
	13/1/18	—	Improvement of KOEKUIT Road.	
	17/1/18	—	Construction of HIGH LEVEL BRIDGE over STEENBEEK at U.21.d.03. Sheet 28.	
	18/1/18 to 22/1/18	—	Continued to carry Infantry in File. Continued work on Accommodation for Infantry in CORPS DEFENSIVE LINE	
	22/1/18	—	Repaired WINTENDRIFT BRIDGE at U.20.b.7.3. Sheet 20.	
	23/1/18	—	Erected 2 Machine Gun Emplacement at PASCAL FARM at U.12.d. Sheet 20.	

Army Form C. 2118.

WAR DIARY
or
INTELLIGENCE SUMMARY.

(Erase heading not required.)

Place	Date	Hour	Summary of Events and Information	Remarks and references to Appendices
B.6.c.8.2. Sheet. 20.	23/1/18	-	Constructs M.G.E. Railway Embankment at U.17a.1.5. Sheet. 20.	
	23/1/18 to 29/1/18	-	Continued work on Infantry Accommodation & Corps DEFENSIVE LINE in U.17.c. and U.16.b. Sheet 20.	
	30/1/18	-	Moved to CROMBEKE AREA. Location WAYENBURG CAMP. X.13.6.E.2. Sheet 19.	
	31/1/18	-	Rest and Training.	

[signature]
O.C. 80th Field Co. R.E.

WAR DIARY
or
INTELLIGENCE SUMMARY.

Army Form C. 2118.

80th Field Coy R.E.

16

VK 27

Place	Date	Hour	Summary of Events and Information	Remarks and references to Appendices
Sheet 19 X 13.c.8.2	1/2/18 to 8/2/18	—	Training	
	9/2/18	—	The Company entrained at PROVEN Station for move to Fifth Army area by statistical train	
ST QUENTIN 1/100,000	10/2/18	6.0 a.m.	Arrived NOYON STATION detrained and proceed to TARLEFESSE by road route. (ST QUENTIN 1/100,000.)	
	10/2/18	8 a.m.	Arrived TARLEFESSE	
	11/2/18	—	Training	
	12/2/18	—	Move to COMMENCHON. Coy H.Q. Sheet 70E/F.8.b.4.8.	
	13/2/18	—	No 4 Section moved to GOLANCOURT. to work on AERODROME	
			82n Squadron R.F.C. - Billets at VILLETTE Sheet 660./P.18.a.67	
	14/2/18	—	Commenced work on RIFLE RANGE. Sheet 70E/F7	
	17/3/18	—	Commenced work on BATHS at CAILLOUEL and COMMENCHON	
	19/2/18	—	Completed Baths at CAILLOUEL and COMMENCHON	
	19/2/18	—	No 2 Section moved to ABBECOURT to work on ITALIAN LABOUR CORPS CAMP at Sheet 70E/L.16.a.5.5.	

Army Form C. 2118.

WAR DIARY
or
INTELLIGENCE SUMMARY.
(Erase heading not required.)

Instructions regarding War Diaries and Intelligence Summaries are contained in F. S. Regs., Part II and the Staff Manual respectively. Title pages will be prepared in manuscript.

Place	Date	Hour	Summary of Events and Information	Remarks and references to Appendices
ST. QUENTIN.	19/2/18	—	No 3 Section moved to CUGNY for work on CAMP FOR ITALIAN LABOUR CORPS at Sheet 66D / R 20.d.6.3.	
	20/2/18	—	Commenced work on HUTMENTS and CAMPS at. ABBECOURT – Sheet 70E.L.10.a.S.5. RUE DE CAUMONT – "70E/F.3.d.6.2. CUGNY. Sheet 66.D/R.20.d.6.3.	
	27/2/18		Continued work on Camps as above.	
	28/2/18		Concentrated 3 Sections at ABBECOURT. Sheet 70E/L.10.a.S.5 for work on Bridge over River OISE at Sheet 70E/L.17.a.7.6.	

Roger Toure
for Major
O.C. 20. Fd. Coy RE.

18th Div.

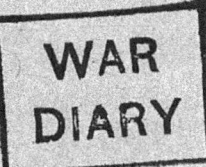

80th FIELD COMPANY, R.E.

M A R C H

1 9 1 8

WAR DIARY
or
INTELLIGENCE SUMMARY

(Erase heading not required.)

Army Form C. 2118

Instructions regarding War Diaries and Intelligence Summaries are contained in F.S. Regs., Part II. and the Staff Manual respectively. Title Pages will be prepared in manuscript.

Place	Date	Hour	Summary of Events and Information	Remarks and references to Appendices
COMMENCEMENT ST. QUENTIN / PERONNE	Nov 1st/1918	8. am	No 1/3 Section moved to ABBECOURT	
	1st		Commenced work on "Infantry to tank" Bridge on R. OISE at ABBECOURT	
	2nd		No 1 . 2 . 3 Section worked on Bridge at ABBECOURT	
	3rd		Bridge Completed	
	4th		No 1 Section returned to CONNECTIN for work on ITALIAN LABOUR CORPS CAMP at RUE DE GAUMONT	
			No 3 Section returned to CUGNY for work on ITALIAN LABOUR CORPS CAMP	
			No 2 " " returned to work on ITALIAN LABOUR CORPS CAMP at ABBECOURT	
	10th		Company moved to Forward Areas with HQ. and Transport at ROUEZ	
ROUEZ.			No 1 Sect at FLAVY – LE – MARTEL.	
			" 2 " " REMIGNY	
			" 3 " " "	
			" 4 " " MENNESSIS	
	11th		No 1. Sect Commenced work on repairs to REMIGNY – MENNESSIS Rd.	
	15 to 20		" 2. 3. 4 Sect works in BATTLE ZONE. left sector.	
			Continued work as above	

WAR DIARY
or
INTELLIGENCE SUMMARY
(Erase heading not required.)

Army Form C. 2118

Place	Date	Hour	Summary of Events and Information	Remarks and references to Appendices
ROUEZ.	21/3/18	5.30 a.m.	Received order to MAN BATTLE POSITIONS. - Coy. less HQ. and Transport moved to position of assembly in BOIS. DE. HELLOT. W. of TIENNESSIS.	
		5.30 p.m.	HQ. and Transport moved to COMMENCHON.	
		11 p.m.	Remainder of Coy. moved to ROUEZ. CAMP. (Casualty. 1. O.R. wounded)	
	22/3/18	10 p.m.	Coy. in Reserve to 53. Inf. Bde.	
			Coy. evacuated ROUEZ CAMP. (Casualties Z. O.R.)	
			Took up position in ROUEZ - VIRY. NOVROEUIL RD.	
			HQ. Transport moved to BABOEUF.	
	23/3/18.	7 am	No. 3 & 4 Section went in support to 53 Inf. Bde in embankment W. of Civin Rd. at ROUEZ.	
			200* W. of R. L. Rouez.	
			No. 1 & Sub. being in Reserve at EMBANKMENT in ROUEZ - LE CAISNEL RD.	
		4 pm.	No. 3 & Section took up position on Ridge 500* W. of ROUEZ. preventing enemy - attack	
		6 pm.	No. 3 & " Enemy attacked. Enemy. completely knocked down. any flanks gun	
			way.	
		7 pm.	No. 3 & 4 Sect. rejoined Company in ROUEZ - LE CAISNEL RD.	
			(Casualties Z Officers. 1. O.R. Killed)	
		9 pm.	Company retired to a position in VILLEQUIER - AUMONT RD.	
		12 Mdn.	" " " RUE DE CAUMONT.	
			Casualties 1. O.R. Missing believed killed. - 10. O.R. wounded. - 1. O.R. wounded Missing	

WAR DIARY or INTELLIGENCE SUMMARY

Army Form C. 2118

(Erase heading not required.)

Instructions regarding War Diaries and Intelligence Summaries are contained in F.S. Regs., Part II. and the Staff Manual respectively. Title Pages will be prepared in manuscript.

Place	Date	Hour	Summary of Events and Information	Remarks and references to Appendices
	24/3/18	1 a.m.	Arrived at BETHANCOURT.	
		6 a.m.	Left BETHANCOURT. arrived k/BABOEUF about 9.30 a.m.	
		11.30 a.m.	Proceeded k/MAILLOEUL to assist 54 Inf Bde in Consolidation of village.	
		11.30 p.m.	Arrived k/BABOEUF. – Transport moved to THIESCOURT. Coy moved k/VARESNES.	
	25/3/18	1.30 a.m.	Arrived VARESNES.	
		9.30 a.m.	Commenced building Footbridge over R. OISE.	
	26/3/18	4 a.m.	Demolished Bridge over OISE CANAL. – Transport moved to MARCQUE – EGLISE.	
		5 a.m.	L/H VARESNES. – proceeded k/CAISNES. – Transport moved k/ESTREES. ST. DENIS.	
		5 p.m.	Left CAISNES proceeded to AUDIGNICOURT.	
	27/3/18	4 a.m.	Left AUDIGNICOURT. proceeded to LA COQUERELLE Fm. ST AUBIN.	
	29/3/18	5 a.m.	Left ST. AUBIN. proceeded by LORRY to GENTELLES.	
	30/3/18	–	Worked on defences of GENTELLES.	
	31/3/18	–	" " " "	
			Casualties 2. O.R. wounded in Patrols.	

(Signed) Major R.E.
Ly F4 Ly
10.4.18.

18th Div.

80th FIELD COMPANY, R.E.

A P R I L

1 9 1 8

WAR DIARY
or
INTELLIGENCE SUMMARY.

Army Form C. 2118.

10 Field Company 29
Vol 1918
April 1918

Place	Date	Hour	Summary of Events and Information	Remarks and references to Appendices
GENTELLES	1/4	—	Company moved from VILLAGE to N.E. Corner of BOIS DE GENTELLES T.11. c. 5.6 Sheet 62 D	
AMIENS /100,000	2/4	—	WIRING DEFENCES of HANGARD WOOD. U 23 b d. (Sheet 62D)	
	3/4	—	— Ditto — Ditto	
	4/4	—	Digging Fire Positions and Copse in U 21 d. and U 22 d.	
	5/4	—	WIRING — GENTELLES — CACHY — VILLERS-BRETONNEUX SWITCH	
	6/12	—	— Do — — Do —	
	4/13	—	— Do — Canadian 8 O.R's	
	13/4	—	Moved to AMIENS. Coy HQr. at ECOLE NORMALE BOULEVARDE CIRATRE AUDUN	
	15/4	—	TRANSPORT at SALEUX.	
	24/4	—	Rest and Training	
	24/4	—	No 3 Section marches to Brigade Camp (S.9.b.) Sheet 62 D and works	
	26/4	—	in constructing Cook houses — latrines etc	
		—	No 3 section rejoined Company at AMIENS	
AVELESGES	26/4	7 pm	Left AMIENS proceeded by Motor Route to AVELESGES. DIEPPE 1/100,000	
DIEPPE 1/100,000	27/4	5 am	Arrived AVELESGES	
	28/4		Rest and TRAINING.	
	30/4			

Captain Major RE
OC 10 Fd Coy RE

Army Form C. 2118.

80th Sutherlands

Vol 30

WAR DIARY
or
INTELLIGENCE SUMMARY.
(Erase heading not required.)

Instructions regarding War Diaries and Intelligence Summaries are contained in F. S. Regs., Part II. and the Staff Manual respectively. Title pages will be prepared in manuscript.

Place	Date	Hour	Summary of Events and Information	Remarks and references to Appendices
AVELUYES G.H.Q at 9.C.5.4 Sh 62.E	1/5/18	—	TRAINING — P.T. Bile rill and initial Arms — Rnts Parade etc	
	2/5/18	—	" " Dtto	
	3/5/18	—	" " Relieved of Brigade Ceremonial Parade	
	4/5/18	—	Transport moved to ARGOEUVES	
—do—	5.V.18	—	Company rests all day.	
	6.V.18	—	Company entrained on WARLUS — CAMP EN — AMEINOIS Ro at 9.30 am arrived at CONTAY at 4.30 pm. moved by road unit to WARLOY	
May 6/18 7	7.V.18	—	Company H.Q. at Shet 57d. V.24.a 6.4 Transport Lines at " 62d. C.3.d.	
		—	Took over work in LAVIEVILLE SECTOR from 517 Fd Cy R.E. Commenced work on Forward Ar: Htrs Right L/h Support Ams Continued work on Bn Htrs and Communical strengthening Collers in LAVIEVILLE	
	8.V.18 13 12.V.18	—	Camouflage CRATER + AMIENS- ALBERT Ro. Continued work on An Htrs - strengthing Collers in LAVIEVILLE	
	13.V.18	—	Work on Construction of Bn Htrs as above	
	14.V.18	—	Ditto — can Subways Wyle Jumpinny YARRA, TR.	

Army Form C. 2118.

WAR DIARY
or
INTELLIGENCE SUMMARY.
(Erase heading not required.)

Instructions regarding War Diaries and Intelligence Summaries are contained in F. S. Regs., Part II. and the Staff Manual respectively. Title pages will be prepared in manuscript.

Place	Date	Hour	Summary of Events and Information	Remarks and references to Appendices
	16/5	—	Finding defensive positions, supervised digging of Communication Trenches, Section of Coy in N.Co. Shelter in forward Sector and Construction of Support Bn HQrs and Reg. Aid Post	
	17/5		— D.ITO	
	18/5		— Ditto	
	19/5		— D.ITO	
	20/5		— D.ITO	
	21/5		⎱ heavy Forward defences — LAVIEVILLE SECTOR	
	22/5		⎰	
	23/5		— Rest —	
	24/5		— Rest and Training	
	25/5		— Rest and Training	
	26/5			
	27/5		⎱ Warm Southern Tunnel WARLOY SECTOR	
	28/5	⎰	Supervising Infantry took a Begin preparing Out Line	
			WARLOY SYSTEM	

Duncan Napier(?)
O.C. 80th Field Co. B.E.F

WAR DIARY or INTELLIGENCE SUMMARY

Army Form C. 2118.

8th Army Troops Vol 31

Place	Date	Hour	Summary of Events and Information	Remarks and references to Appendices
WARLOY (Coy HQrs at V.24.a.6.a. Sheet 57D)	1/6/18 to 4/6/18		Erection of large English shelters for Divisional A.I. Op. at U.21.c. (57D)	
	5/6/18		3 Sections — Ditto —	
	6/6/18		1 " proceeded to Divisional Reception Camp Molliens-au-Bois. Erecting Hutments — Cookhouses — Latrines etc.	
	6/6/18 to 8/6/18		3 Sections on Div. Reception Camp. 1 " " D.HQ.	
	9/6/18 to 15/6/18		2 Sections on D.HQ. 1 " Div. Reception Camp 1 " Tactical Wiring on Henencourt System.	
	16/6 to 26/6		Relieved 79th Field Coy RE in LEFT BRIGADE SECTOR. Work on S.A. Det. Pde. Wiring. Erection of Shelters. Improvements to C.T.s & Front Line — Making Battle Zone Emplacements — Mobile Charges etc. preparatory to MINOR OPERATIONS.	

Army Form C. 2118.

WAR DIARY
or
INTELLIGENCE SUMMARY.
(Erase heading not required.)

Instructions regarding War Diaries and Intelligence Summaries are contained in F. S. Regs., Part II. and the Staff Manual respectively. Title pages will be prepared in manuscript.

Place	Date	Hour	Summary of Events and Information	Remarks and references to Appendices
	Continued			
	27/6	—	Manned Battle Sector (Left Sector WARLOY SYSTEM) to practice positions.	
	29/6 to 30/6/16		Relieved 92nd Field Coy R.E. in Right Brigade Sector. Worked on improvements to MELBOURNE STRONG POINT and DIVISIONAL MAIN DEFENCE LINE.	

Bedford
Major R.E.
O.C. 9th Field Coy R.E.

Army Form C. 2118.

80 4th Coy R.E. Vol 3D

WAR DIARY
or
INTELLIGENCE SUMMARY.
(Erase heading not required.)

Instructions regarding War Diaries and Intelligence Summaries are contained in F.S. Regs., Part II. and the Staff Manual respectively. Title pages will be prepared in manuscript.

Place	Date	Hour	Summary of Events and Information	Remarks and references to Appendices
WARLOY. (Coy. HQrs. at V22 a 6.4. Sheet 57 D.)	1.7/16 to 11.7/16		Improving MELBOURNE TRENCH.	
	12.7/16		Company moved to LA CHAUSSEE for training.	
	13.7/16 29.7/16		TRAINING.	
HEILLY.	29.7/16 31.7/16		Company moved to HEILLY found section and took over billets of 8th AUSTRALIAN FIELD Coy. at I.5 a.2.2 (62.D). Horselines at C.28 x.9.6 (62.D). Improved billets and took over work in the line from 14th AUSTRALIAN FIELD Coy.	Mn. CoyR. 8. OC O3rd Fd.Coy.R.E. Mn. CoyR. 8. OC O3rd Fd.Coy.R.E.

18th DIVISION.
ENGINEERS

80th FIELD COMPANY R.E.

AUGUST 1918

WAR DIARY
INTELLIGENCE SUMMARY

Army Form C. 2118.

80 4th Coy R.E.
9th (33rd?) Div.

Place	Date	Hour	Summary of Events and Information	Remarks and references to Appendices
HEILLY	1.8.18		No 4. SECTION at HORSE LINES at C.29 d.9.6 (62 D)	
			No 2 SECTION moved to forward Billets at J.23 d.7.2. (62 D)	
			No 3 SECTION " " " J.22 d.3.4. "	
			No 1 SECTION and COMPANY HQ moved to J.27 a.4.8. "	
	2.8.18		No 3 SECTION constructed 2 C TYPE SHELTERS for Right BTN. COMMAND POST at K.25.6.1.8. (62 D)	
	5.8.18		Nos 1, 2 & 4 SECTIONS worked on dugouts at K.20.a.45. (62 D) for BRIGADE COMMAND POST and RIGHT BTN. COMMAND POST.	
	6.8.18		On nights of 6 – 8.8.18 the above works were carried on by the ENEMY along with parties working on them.	
	6.8.18		COMPANY HQ and Nos 1, 2 & 3 SECTIONS moved to new billets at J.14.C.5.7.	
	6.8.18 7.8.18		Prepared wire and formed forward dumps of R.E. MATERIALS.	
	8.8.18.		Constructed STRONG POINTS at K.20.b.75 and K.20. a.05.70.	
	9.8.18		All sections and attached Platoon erected 1050 yards wire Apron fence in K.21 a.b.d. & K.27.b.	
	10.8.18		COMPANY MOVED to WARLOY	
WARLOY Coy HQ rs at V.2.a.6.t. (57 D)	11.8.18		Taking over work from 57627th FIELD COY	
	12.8.18 13.8.18		In front of Mill Butte AUSTRALIA ST. — FORWARD TRACKS MAKING FORWARD TRACKS, BRIDGING TRENCHES &c.	

Army Form C. 2118.

WAR DIARY
or
INTELLIGENCE SUMMARY.

(Erase heading not required.)

Instructions regarding War Diaries and Intelligence Summaries are contained in F. S. Regs., Part II. and the Staff Manual respectively. Title pages will be prepared in manuscript.

Place	Date	Hour	Summary of Events and Information	Remarks and references to Appendices
WARLOY.	14/8/18 to 20/8/18		Making Forward Overland Tracks including Bridging Trestles.	
	21/8/18		Preparation of Infantry Footbridges for use in Operations.	
	22/8	9.30am	Arrive at R. ANCRE. ( ) with 2 Bridging Wagons unloaded same at — in Conjunction with	
			Commence to cut Footbridges on R. ANCRE in Conjunction with attack of 54 Inf. Bde.	
		5.15am	Commence erection of Trestle Bridge suitable for Infantry in France on R. ANCRE at DERNANCOURT. (Steel Trestle Bridge suitable for Infantry in France)	
		9am	Commence erection of Trestle Bridge on R. ANCRE at E16a.2.7. and B.16 a.4.8.	
		3pm	Above Bridge Completed.	
			During the day Reconnaissance parties were out searching for WELLS — WATERSUPPLY — TRAPS — ROAD MINES, etc.	

WAR DIARY
or
INTELLIGENCE SUMMARY

Army Form C. 2118.

Place	Date	Hour	Summary of Events and Information	Remarks and references to Appendices
	23/8	9 a.m.	in Capture Area. Commenced reliefs	
			Casualties. 1 Officer. 5 O.R. Wounded.	
			9 O.R. Killed	
			11 O.R. Wounded.	
		4 p.m.	Two Coys reliefs bridge on R. ANCRE at E.10.D.7.1	
LAVIEVILLE	24/8	—	Worked on Strong Points E.11.c.2.5 & E.11.b.4.2. E.5.b.8.5.	
			650 x Barbed wire fence erected.	
			Coy turned to V.10.c.5.8. (Sht. 62.D. N.E.)	
			Two 1st 2nd Sections worked on approaches to Bridges on R. ANCRE	
			at E.16.a.2.7. and E.16.a.4.7.	
	25/8		Re: erecting 12 Footbridges on ANCRE between ALBERT FUNKER TILL (Sht. 62 D N E)	
			Company moved to E.10.d.5.8. (62.D N.E.)	
			Engaged in erection of Storage Tanks from water supply.	
	26/8		Company erecting HORSE WATERING POINTS at E.16.a. (62 D N.E)	
			and erection of Storage Tanks from water supply.	

WAR DIARY
INTELLIGENCE SUMMARY

Army Form C. 2118.

Place	Date	Hour	Summary of Events and Information	Remarks and references to Appendices
	27/8			
	28/8		On 26/8/16. Company moves to X.23 central Caterpillar Valley, 57c. No 4 Section were employed with Advance Guard unit. 54 Inf. Bde. Remainder with in GUILLEMONT.	
Sheet 57c. 1/40,000			No 4 Sect. Billeted at BERNAFAY WOOD (S.28.b.5.7)	
BERNAFAY WOOD	29/8		Company moves to S.28.b.5.7. (Sheet 57c). Continue work in improving huts, shelters in GUILLEMONT.	
	30/8		Ditto. No 2 Section proceeded to work on reconnaissance works in COMBLES.	
COMBLES	31/8		Continue work on hut shelters in COMBLES.	

(signed) Edgar Maynel?
O.C. 80 Field Coy, RE.

WAR DIARY or INTELLIGENCE SUMMARY

Army Form C. 2118.

(Erase heading not required.)

Place	Date	Hour	Summary of Events and Information	Remarks and references to Appendices
BERNAFAY WOOD	1/9/18	—	Company at S28b.6.8. Sheet 57c.S.W.	
	2/9		Transport at S.20.a. — Work WATER SUPPLY COMBLES — Ditto	
COMBLES	3/9		Move to COMBLES to T.22.c.5.7. Engaged on Water Supply and Erection of D.H.Qrs	
	4/9		Worked on Water Supply COMBLES and Erection of D.H.Qrs D.H.Q. — Ditto —	
	5/9			
	5/9		Move to LEUZE WOOD T.27a.3.7 with Transport Lines T.26b.	
	6/9 to 12/9	Various	Rest and Training	
AIZECOURT-LE-BAS	13/9		No. 2 & 3 Sections move to AIZECOURT-LE-BAS D.18.c.S.3 Sheet 62.d.N.E. Worked on D.H.Q. LIERAMONT	
	14/9		Erection D.H.Q. LIERAMONT.	
	15/9		No.1 Section move to D.18.c.S.3 Worked on B.H.Q. SAULCOURT	
	16/9		Company H.Q. & Transport move to D.18.c.S.3 with Transport lines at D.16.b. N.H.Qrs. LIERAMONT LIERAMONT B.H.Q. SAULCOURT	
	17/9		Work. — Ditto —	

WAR DIARY
or
INTELLIGENCE SUMMARY.

Army Form C. 2118.

Place	Date	Hour	Summary of Events and Information	Remarks and references to Appendices
AIZICOURT-LE BAS	18/9	4 am	Company moved forward to ST EMILIE in preparation for work in conjunction with operations of 54th Inf. Bde. 2 Sections attached to 54th Inf. Bde. for Consolidation of GREEN LINE. 2 " " under C.R.E. employed on work Suppl. Casualties 9 O.R. WOUNDED.	
	19/9	4.30 pm	Returned to Camp at AIZICOURT-LE-BAS. No. 2 Section continues work in water Supply RONSSOY. Remainder of Coy. RESTING.	
	20/9		No. 2 Sect. employed on Water Supply, RONSSOY. No. 4 " Buy Water Tank from ST EMILIE - RONSSOY.	
	21/9		2 Sections attached to 54 Inf. Bde. for purpose of Consolidation.	
	22/9		No. 1 & 3 Sections moved forward to vicinity of DUNCAN POST, but were unable to Consolidate owing to this post being taken by the enemy. Returned to Camp at 7am. 3 Casualties. 2 O.R. killed. 1 O.R. wounded.	
	22/9	5 pm	No. 2 & 4 Section Consolidated DUNCAN POST.	

Army Form C. 2118.

WAR DIARY
or
INTELLIGENCE SUMMARY.
(Erase heading not required.)

Instructions regarding War Diaries and Intelligence Summaries are contained in F. S. Regs., Part II. and the Staff Manual respectively. Title pages will be prepared in manuscript.

Place	Date	Hour	Summary of Events and Information	Remarks and references to Appendices
AZICOURT LE BAS	23/9	5 p.m.	No. 2, 3, 4 Sections moved to COMBLES. No. 1 Section engaged in SIGNAL OFFICE for Bn. R.A. at LIERMONT.	
	23/9	5 p.m.	No. 2, 3, 4 Sections moved to COMBLES.	
COMBLES.	24/9	—	Coy. H.Qrs. and Transport moved to COMBLES. lined a ditches	
	25/9	—	Company and Transport lines in COMBLES at T.28.a.3.6. Sheet 57c. S.W.	
			Work on erection of Div. H.Qrs. in COMBLES.	
	26/9		Continue work on Div. H.Qrs.	
	27/9	10 a.m.	Company attended Ceremonial Parade at COMBLES.	
NURLU.	27/9	2 p.m.	Company moved to NURLU. — HQrs at D.13.a.5.4. — 62c.	
	28/9	4 a.m.	No. 4 Section moves to EPEHY AREA. E.4.a.2.6. Bn. 62c.	
	29/9	5 p.m.	No. 4 " " "QUID POST. F.14.a.0.8. Bn. 62c	
			Nos. 1, 2, 3. Sects moved to GUYENCOURT. E.3.a.7.6. " 62c.	
			This section was detailed to accompany LIAISON FORCE work in	
	29/9	6 a.m.	Conjunction with 27 Div. U.S. Army who were attacking the HINDENBERG	
			LINE S. VENDHUILLE. This section reached F.11.d.8.5. and were	
			unable to proceed further.	
	29/9	5 p.m.	Reassembled at F.14.a.0.8. — rejoined Coy. at Canal 30/9/18.	

Army Form C. 2118.

WAR DIARY
or
INTELLIGENCE SUMMARY.
(Erase heading not required)

Instructions regarding War Diaries and Intelligence Summaries are contained in F.S. Regs., Part II. and the Staff Manual respectively. Title pages will be prepared in manuscript.

80 Fd Coy R.E.
Vol 35

Place	Date	Hour	Summary of Events and Information	Remarks and references to Appendices
BEAUCOURT SUR HALLUE	1918 Oct. 1.		TRANSPORT moved to CATERPILLAR VALLEY.	
	2.		" " to BEAUCOURT-SUR-HALLUE.	
			" " " from "	
			SECTIONS moved by Motor Lorry from GUYENCOURT to "	
	Oct 3. to Oct 16.		TRAINING and REST.	
NURLU.	Oct. 16.		TRANSPORT MOVED TO MAMETZ.	
	-17.		COMPANY and "TRANSPORT" detailed at POZIAINVILLE and moved to NURLU AREA returning to ROISEL	
			CYCLISTS moved by ROAD to NURLU AREA	
SERAIN.	-18.		TRANSPORT and CYCLISTS moved by road to SERAIN.	
			COMPANY and TRANSPORT + CYCLISTS moved by Bus. to SERAIN.	
	-20.		Reconnoitred RAILWAY LEVEL CROSSING at K 29. a. 81. (SHEET. 57/B.)	
MAUROIS	-21.		Moved to MAUROIS.	
LE CATEAU	-22.		Nos 1 + 3 Section moved to LE CATEAU.	
	-23.		Nº 4 Section constructed FOOTBRIDGE over RICHEMONT RIVER at K 23.6.26.	
			OPERATIONS	
			Nº 3 SECTION constructed TRESTLE BRIDGE over the RICHEMONT RIVER at RICHEMONT Mill. K 23.a.40	
			Nº 1. + Reconnoitred ROADS, WELLS, MINES etc. in Area taken by 57TH INF BDE. (K. 29, 23, 24	
			-1, 18, 13, 7, 8, 2, 3, and F 27, 28)	
			Nos 2 + 4 Sections moved to LE CATEAU	
			TRANSPORT and HQ moved to LE CATEAU.	
	-24.			
	-25.		Nos 1, 2, + 4 Sections Continued reconnaissance of Roads + Tracks, found hurs, holes + wires)	
	-26.			
	-27.			
	-28.			
	-29.		Sinking men Improved Defence line in front of BOUSIES.	
	-30.			
	-31.			

CASUALTIES Nil.

W.M. Cox R.E.
for OC Nº 80 Fd Coy R.E.

WAR DIARY
or
INTELLIGENCE SUMMARY.
(Erase heading not required.)

Army Form C.2118.

8074 Coy RE
Vol 36

Place	Date	Hour	Summary of Events and Information	Remarks and references to Appendices
LE CATEAU	Nov /18	1.	Nos 1 + 3 Sections Constructing Bde. H.Q. (2 C.TYPE Shelters) at F.24.C.82. (57B)	CASUALTIES. Nil.
		2.	" 2 + 4 " " 2.BTN. H.Q.s ROBERSART.	
		3.	No 4. SECTION Completed a Structure of BTN. H.Q.	
		4.	No 1, 2 + 3 Section noted grounds & bivouacs at L.3 Central (57B.)	
		4.	No 4. Section " " " " " " "	
			OPERATIONS:-	
			No 1. SECTION Reconnoitred Water Supply + prep. of A16 A.49. (57B.) and opening at A.23 d.2.9	
			No 2 " Reconnaissance for Points t/o and Walk to PREUX-AU-BOIS.	
			No 3 " Examined roads in PREUX-AU-BOIS area + cleared Rd.	
			No 4 " Hatton LE QUESNOY — LANDRECIES Rd. Bretro Indian trails — PREUX-AU-BOIS.	
			No 1. Sectn Erected Lone debus Point at A16 A.49.	
			No 2 + 3 Reconnoitre roads etc in FORET de MORMAL.	
			No 4 " Reconnoitre crossing of RIVER SAMBRE at SASSIGNIES.	
		5.	COMPANY moved to PREUX-AU-BOIS.	
		5.	No 2 SECTION Constructed foot bridge across R. SAMBRE at PONT-AU-BOIS.	
		6.	No 4 " " " " " " SASSIGNIES.	
		7.	No 2 " Opened 222 FIELD Coy RE & On-thielch trestle bridge at SASSIGNIES.	
			COMPANY moved to HACHETTE. (57A)	
HACHETTE		8.	Nos 1/2.3 + 4 SECTIONS Constructed Construction of CORDUROY Road & Pontoon Bridge at B.29 Central (Shot 57A)	
		9.	" " " " " " Bridge to carry Lorries at B.27 Central + Bruneur to west	

Army Form C. 2118.

WAR DIARY
or
INTELLIGENCE SUMMARY.
(Erase heading not required.)

Instructions regarding War Diaries and Intelligence Summaries are contained in F. S. Regs., Part II and the Staff Manual respectively. Title pages will be prepared in manuscript.

Army Form C. 2118.

Place	Date	Hour	Summary of Events and Information	Remarks and references to Appendices
HACHETTE	Nov./18			
	10-16.		Constructed lorry Bridge at B.27 Cent. (sheet 57 A).	
	16-17.		Lifted & reconstructed, & carry lorries, Corduroy road which has been constructed on the 8th & 9th.	
	18.		Company moved to MADRIS. (sheet 57 B) {Transport & stores units} {Remainder}	
	19.		" " SERAIN. & rest units.	
	20-30.		Nos 1,2,3 & 4 sections (stores) did dull demolitions on S.A.M./Ber. Salvage and Repairs billets in SERAIN.	CASUALTIES. NIL.

[Signature]
O.C. 80th Feb Co. R.E.

Army Form C. 2118.

INTELLIGENCE SUMMARY.

(Erase heading not required.)

80 Z⁰ Coy RE
9R 37

Place	Date	Hour	Summary of Events and Information	Remarks and references to Appendices
SERAIN	DEC. R/18		(VALENCIENNES 1/100 ODD)	
	1-12-18		Company employed on Mine	
	10-12-18		(a) Destruction of "DUD" SHELLS, BOMBS and GRENADES	
			(b) Repairs to BILLETS in SERAIN and BEAUREVOIR	
	10.12.18		Company moves to WALINCOURT.	
WALINCOURT	11.12.18		Company employed in { Destruction of "Dud" Shells etc. and demolition of Dugouts.	
	31.12.18		{ Repairs to Billets in WALINCOURT & SELVIGNY.	

[signature]
O/C. 80TH FIELD COY. R.E.

Army Form C. 2118.

WAR DIARY
or
INTELLIGENCE SUMMARY.

(Erase heading not required.)

80TH FIELD COY. RE

WC 38

Instructions regarding War Diaries and Intelligence Summaries are contained in F. S. Regs., Part II. and the Staff Manual respectively. Title pages will be prepared in manuscript.

Place	Date	Hour	Summary of Events and Information	Remarks and references to Appendices
WALINCOURT.	JAN /19		Company employed in { Detaching of DUD shells. Dismantling Dugouts. Repairs to Billets in WALINCOURT & SELVIGNY. Fitting out Coy. H.Q. at SELVIGNY. }	

J M. Capt. RE.
86 Feb '19. Coy RE.

WAR DIARY
or
INTELLIGENCE SUMMARY.

Army Form C. 2118.

80 Fd Coy R.E.

Place	Date	Hour	Summary of Events and Information	Remarks and references to Appendices
WALINCOURT	1/2/19 – 28/2/19		Company Hdqrs at WALINCOURT. Engaged on Demolition of "DUD" Shells. Improvements to Billets	Sheet 57 B 1/20,000

Asgad Major RE
O Bo Fd Cy RE

WAR DIARY
INTELLIGENCE SUMMARY

Army Form C. 2118.

80 Fd Coy R.E.

(Erase heading not required.)

Place	Date	Hour	Summary of Events and Information	Remarks and references to Appendices
WALINCOURT	1 Novr 15		At Walincourt	
	15 Novr			
	17" "		At CAUDRY	
	31 " "		VALENCIENNES. Company engaged in Repairs to Billets. Demolition of "Dud" Shells. Company engaged in Erection of XIII Corps Packet Structures & "Dud" Shells. Repairs to Billets. ORDNANCE. I.C.S.	

Ledgard Major R.E.
O.C. 80 Fd Coy R.E.

Army Form C. 2118.

WAR DIARY
or
INTELLIGENCE SUMMARY.
(Erase heading not required.)

80 Fd Coy R.E.

Place	Date	Hour	Summary of Events and Information	Remarks and references to Appendices
CAUDRY	1st April to 30th April		Or CAUDRY — VALENCIENNES 12/100,000 — Company engaged in checking all stores on Coy. Charge & cleaning same. All company transport & harness, etc. overhauled & oiled.	

R. A. Fitton
Ft Lt. R.E.
o/c. D.C. 80th Field Coy. R.E.